The Art of Marketing Jesus

The Art of Marketing Jesus

Unleashing the Power of the Gospel
through the Lives of Everyday Believers

Robert Wachter

RESOURCE *Publications* · Eugene, Oregon

THE ART OF MARKETING JESUS
Unleashing the Power of the Gospel through the Lives
of Everyday Believers

Resource Publications
An Imprint of Wipf and Stock Publishers
199 W. 8th Ave., Suite 3
Eugene, OR 97401

www.wipfandstock.com

PAPERBACK ISBN: 978-1-7252-8169-1
HARDCOVER ISBN: 978-1-7252-8168-4
EBOOK ISBN: 978-1-7252-8170-7

JULY 13, 2021

Contents

INTRODUCTION | vii

Chapter 1   PUBLIC RELATIONS | 1
Chapter 2   ATTRACTION MARKETING | 13
Chapter 3   BRAND IMAGE | 29
Chapter 4   BRAND VALUES | 45
Chapter 5   BRAND PROMISE | 59
Chapter 6   BRAND INTEGRITY | 74
Chapter 7   BE LOVED | 88
Chapter 8   BELONG | 101
Chapter 9   BE YOU | 115
Chapter 10   BRAND STORY | 128

NOTES | 142

About the Author | 144

Introduction

JESUS IS THE MOST attractive person in human history. Professional fishermen dropped everything to follow Him. Social outcasts were transformed into outspoken ambassadors; sinners, repulsed by other religious leaders, were drawn to Jesus by the scores; and two thousand years later, even in our modern culture, Jesus is still attracting people in numbers that can't be counted. Only now, because Jesus is no longer here in the flesh, the process of attracting people happens largely through the lives of everyday believers.

However, attracting others to Jesus may not seem like a viable option for some people. I spent many years battling fractures in my soul that prevented me from experiencing spiritual freedom. I was either dealing with serious mental health issues, fighting my way through addictive bondages, or buried underneath destructive feelings of condemnation. I had a personal relationship with Jesus and desperately wanted my light to shine, but spiritual victory often seemed elusive. It was only through the process of renewing my mind to the unadulterated gospel of grace that brought true spiritual victory in my life.

Although I was caught in the subtle influences of religion that resulted in feelings of rejection from God, others have come to the faulty conclusion that their performance is keeping them in right standing with God. This produces the unintended consequences of self-righteousness and judgmental attitudes that render the believer ineffective at reflecting the heart of God. The fastest way to turn people away from wanting to know more about Jesus is through an attitude that looks down on others. Therefore, we must understand why this happens and free ourselves from the Achilles heel that distracts people from seeing the true Jesus through our lives.

After reading the gospel accounts, Mahatma Gandhi, one of the most well-known practicing Hindus in recent history, wanted to learn more about Jesus. One Sunday morning, Gandhi visited a Christian church located in Calcutta, India. Unfortunately, however, like many people who are curious about Jesus today, he did not have the best experience dealing with Christians. Gandhi was stopped at the sanctuary doors and told the church was only for high-caste Indians and white people. Understandably, the experience left a bad taste in Gandhi's mouth. "I like your Christ; I do not like your Christians. Your Christians are so unlike your Christ."

We may push people away in other ways today, but the impact is the same. We are often quick to attack people on social media for their behaviors or political beliefs, not realizing that we are pushing them further away from Jesus. We often pretend that we don't have any problems in our lives, only to make the Christian faith seem entirely unrelatable to hurting people. We may even proclaim our love for the world but refuse to pursue relationships with people who don't share our faith. *The Art of Marketing Jesus* recognizes that we must tackle these problems head on to revitalize the connection between humanity and the authentic and captivating person of Jesus.

I first started thinking about how to help believers attract more people to Jesus during the planning stages of launching Imagine Church. As a marketing executive for many years prior to entering full-time ministry, I thought about how some of the methodologies used to clarify the value of name brands in the business world could be used to help deliver people from religious and spiritual bondages. I immediately went to work creating a powerful and easy-to-understand spiritual growth process that has helped many believers internalize the life-giving promises of the new covenant and produce an abundance of love, joy, and peace in their lives—which is precisely the attitudes and characteristics required to attract people to Jesus.

I've divided this book into three categories. The first part focuses on how God intends to use everyday believers to attract people to Jesus. We are all broken people who need the power of God to transform our lives. The good news is that God specializes in doing extraordinary things through the lives of ordinary people. It doesn't matter how unqualified you may feel today, God will use every difficult experience and broken piece in your life to attract people to Himself. It's often those who come from the most challenging circumstances who have the most impact on others. However, when it comes to the art of marketing Jesus, we must be willing to tell the real story about what God has done in our lives, which means exposing our frailties and failures.

The second part of the book uses intriguing marketing concepts to clarify and articulate the simple message of the gospel. The only way to reflect the true heart of God is to first untangle ourselves from the subtle but deadly influences of religious thinking. The gospel is not based on the conventional wisdom of the world. Instead, it was given to the first-century apostles through divine revelation from the Holy Spirit. We must look at why rules-based living does not work on this side of the cross and challenge old thoughts that do not align with the new covenant. This is the only way to free ourselves from the shackles of religion.

The third part of the book introduces a highly effective grace-based spiritual growth process rooted firmly in the promises of the new covenant. We often get stuck in the performance trap because we put works before the power of grace. This always leads to spiritual frustration and burnout because we are operating on human strength. The spiritual growth process will give you the tools to remain filled with all the fullness of God, integrate your life with other life-giving believers, and teach you how to live victoriously on this side of the cross.

Join me as we begin the journey to freedom from a performance-based religion and start living the abundant life that can only be found in Jesus.

Chapter 1

Public Relations

If I was down to my last dollar, I would spend it on public relations.

BILL GATES[1]

Public relations can be defined as the state of the relationship between the public and a company, organization, or famous person. The two most effective strategies used to drive public relations are known as press conferences and press releases. It might surprise you to learn that Jesus used both methods during His ministry. He certainly relied on different tactical elements to achieve His objectives in the first century, but the fundamental concepts were the same then as they are today.

Every marketing professional understands the importance of controlling the content and timing of messages that reach the public. For example, when a company is preparing for a new product launch or noteworthy personnel change, a great deal of energy goes into controlling when and how the information reaches the public. This is perhaps even more important in the realm of celebrity personalities and politicians. Sending out important information to targeted audiences and conducting damage control are part of the process. The information that does reach the general public, whether good or bad, can leave a lasting impression.

On November 17, 1973, during the height of the Watergate controversy, President Richard Nixon made the tactical mistake of uttering five infamous words during a press conference that would ultimately defame his presidency: "I am not a crook." Those words cemented a shadowy impression about Nixon in the collective mind of the entire country (and the world, for that matter). He intended to affirm the positive, that he's not a crook, but he made the self-imposed mistake of associating himself with crooks. It was like saying, "I don't beat my wife." Not the best moment for Nixon. And, unfortunately for him, it was all too catchy.

More recently, on June 16, 2015, at Trump Tower in New York City, Donald Trump leveraged the power of the press conference to announce his bid to run for the presidency of the United States. Love him or hate him, there's no denying that Trump is a public relations genius. The mere optics of coming down the famous escalator while standing next to Melania Trump, coupled with the controversial words he spoke that day, generated the equivalent of a public relations atomic bomb that reverberated across the entire world. Trump continued to push his message using the national media apparatus as a sounding board throughout the campaign.

In 2016, the *New York Times* published an article that demonstrated the extent to which Trump drove the media narrative. The article cited a study conducted by mediaQuant, a leading firm that computes the dollar value politicians receive from the media, which includes news broadcasts, print stories, and social media reach. The results were astounding. Trump earned a whopping two billion dollars' worth of free media coverage during his campaign and more than doubled his nearest competitor. The article summarized that Trump may have been the most effective candidate in the history of United States politics at earning free media.[2] That's saying a lot coming from the *New York Times*.

Looking back at the campaign, it would seem the public relations strategy worked for Trump—he won the presidency.

When you travel back in time even further and examine how public relations worked in the first century, it's clear that no news cameras or reporters were on the scene that resembled today's media culture. During that time, word-of-mouth testimony was the modern form of "breaking news." As you can imagine, the more credible the witness, the more credible the news story. This was the first-century equivalent of newspapers, social media, and televised news conferences. The Gospels record several ways that Jesus took advantage of every relevant public relations method available at the time. Everything from coordinating important press conferences, to sending out press releases to target audiences, to controlling His publicity through the suppression of certain miracles—we can't deny that Jesus was highly intentional with His public relations strategy.

The Press Conference

When Jesus was about thirty years old, heaven was in the process of orchestrating a spectacular press conference to announce the launch of His public ministry. As the special day approached, John the Baptist, who had become a well-known prophet, was baptizing people in the Jordan River. One day Jesus came to be baptized too. Although John was hesitant, Jesus insisted that John must baptize Him. What happened next was truly remarkable. When Jesus came out of the water, the Holy Spirit descended upon Him in the form of a dove, for everyone to see. If that wasn't incredible enough, the event was followed by a voice that thundered from heaven, for everyone to hear, "You are my Son, whom I love; with you I am well pleased" (Mark 1:11).

There is no denying the dramatics of this scene. It's the only place in the Bible that shows the Father, Son, and Holy Spirit interacting simultaneously. Scholars agree that when God chose to perform notable miraculous signs, such as the burning bush and the parting of the Red Sea, the level of dramatics matched the significance of the spiritual reality being communicated. In this case, ever since Adam took the forbidden fruit in the garden of Eden, the fate of humanity rested on the shoulders of Jesus. Centuries of writings and prophecies spoke about His coming. Israel waited patiently for the glorious day to arrive, but it would happen only in God's sovereign timing. Finally, after waiting hundreds of years, the time had arrived.

After the baptism, Jesus spent the next forty days in the wilderness fasting and preparing for His ministry, the final step before going public with His mission. During the forty days, He endured several temptations from Satan that were meant to derail the mission. Of course, Jesus was victorious over Satan at every turn. At the completion of the fast, Jesus traveled back to His hometown and entered the local synagogue on the Sabbath. Jesus was given the scroll that contained the words from the prophet Isaiah, whereby He located the portion of the Scripture that speaks about the promised Messiah. He then read it aloud to the people: "The Spirit of the Lord is on me, because he has anointed me to proclaim good news to the poor. He has sent me to proclaim freedom for the prisoners and recovery of sight for the blind, to set the oppressed free, to proclaim the year of the Lord's favor" (Luke 4:17–19).

It was not uncommon for a spiritual leader to read Scripture aloud in the synagogue, but what happened next was most remarkable. Jesus handed the scroll back to the attendant then sat down. The eyes of everyone in the building were fastened on Him. The stage was set, the house was packed, and everyone sat on the edge of their seats, waiting to see what Jesus would do next. At which point, Jesus capitalized on the moment with perhaps the most profound words recorded in the Bible: "Today this scripture is fulfilled in your hearing" (Luke 4:21). To underscore the importance of this moment, New Testament scholars agree that Jesus spoke these words to signal the start of His public ministry.

If you think any of these events happened by coincidence, please think again. Jesus chose the most important location in the region, during the most significant Jewish tradition, to announce the commencement of His public mission. He also revealed, in no uncertain terms, that He was the promised Messiah. The press conference was preceded by the Father's miraculous words of affirmation spoken during the baptism. Every detail was orchestrated in sequential order to reinforce the veracity of the press conference and generate maximum exposure among the most influential leaders in the region. We can only imagine the astonishment of the people in attendance, who witnessed the seven-hundred-year-old prophecy come to life.

The Press Release

Another highly effective method used to accomplish public relations is known as the press release, which is a factual document designed to inform the general public about important news. For example, on January 9, 2007, Apple published a press release that announced the launch of the first iPhone. The announcement still exists on Apple's website today, appropriately titled, "Apple Reinvents the Phone with iPhone."[3] Businesses will often hire public relations professionals to create newsworthy stories and then seek to get them published with influential media outlets.

Press releases in the first century were not as they are today. Most people were illiterate and there was no press apparatus or internet to publish information to the masses. Back then, instead of online articles and newspaper stands, information was delivered verbally. If someone needed to communicate important news to another person or group of people, a personal messenger was sent on behalf of the news source. Multiple examples in the Gospels demonstrate exactly how Jesus orchestrated perfectly timed press releases to achieve His ministry goals. One of the most obvious was when Jesus announced His intention to expand His ministry to include the gentile people.

Including gentile (non-Jewish) people into God's redemptive plan may seem natural today, but back then, in the context of the Jewish tradition, the idea was completely absurd. For hundreds of years, it was understood that only people of Jewish heritage could be in covenant with God. However, Jesus was about to reverse that way of thinking in accordance with God's original plan. When God first told Abraham that he would become the father of many nations, the details surrounding the promise also stated that every people group in the world would be blessed through his seed. Jesus reaffirmed that promise with the following statement, "For God so loved *the world* that He gave His one and only Son, that whoever who believes in him shall not perish but have eternal life" (John 3:16).

Jesus spent the first two years of public ministry focused predominantly within two Jewish regions known as Galilee and Judea. Eventually, He implemented more intentional strategies to reach beyond the Jewish boundaries. To get the attention of the gentiles, Jesus needed to penetrate the barriers of culture and send the powerful message that God's redemptive plan included them too. When the time was right, Jesus and the disciples traveled across the Sea of Galilee, where a demon-possessed man confronted them. The demoniac lived among the tombs on the outskirts of an area occupied by the Gerasenes, which was part of a larger collection of cities well-populated by gentiles.

The situation with the demon-possessed man was enormously challenging. The demons drove him to the point of complete lunacy, and nobody was able to contain him, not even with chains. To be clear, no mental hospitals or trained medical teams with the resources to help existed at the time. Nor did the society have the wherewithal to deal with the spiritual nature of the problem. Therefore, the gentile people separated the man from their community and placed him on the outskirts of the region where the tombs were located. The word picture we get from this scenario could not be more striking. The demoniac was a dead man walking in every sense of the term. Furthermore, the gentile people were powerless to deal with the severity of his condition.

No matter how bad a situation may look on the outside, good things always happen when Jesus shows up. In this case, Jesus proceeded to heal the demoniac by removing the unclean spirits out of the man and sending them into nearby pigs. We must pause for a moment to consider the magnitude of this miracle. The demoniac represented the living embodiment of what it means to exist under the control of Satan. However, after just one touch from Jesus, the madman was completely delivered from the power of darkness. He went from being a helpless outcast living among the tombs to a completely normal person. Only now, the man was the living embodiment of the power and love of God. Not surprisingly, when the time came for Jesus to leave the region, the man wanted to go with Him. However, Jesus had a different purpose for his life.

Jesus told the former demoniac, "Go home to your own people and tell them how much the Lord has done for you, and how he has had mercy on you" (Mark 5:19). When the man returned to his hometown, the people were all amazed that he was healed. There was no denying the miraculous nature of the demoniac's turnaround. One can only imagine the surge of belief that spread among the people following such an incredible display of power. The event was designed to send an important message to the gentile people directly from the headquarters of the Jewish Messiah. Every detail, from the crossing of the Sea of Galilee to the deliverance of the demoniac, was used to inform the audience that Satan was no match for Jesus, and that God loved them too. The press release was carefully written in heaven for the expressed purpose of reaching the gentiles, and the former demoniac was the perfect messenger to deliver the good news.

You Are Light

The art of marketing Jesus hinges on the power of the gospel working through the lives of everyday believers. Jesus once said to His followers, "You are the light of the world. A town built on a hill cannot be hidden" (Matthew 5:14). This statement offers profound insight into how God uses ordinary believers to attract others to Jesus. The process of being delivered from the power of darkness and transferred into the kingdom of God creates an expression of heavenly light within the believer that is available for people to see. We have been placed in the unique position to change the eternal outcome of lives based on how we think, live, and impact others. However, many religious barriers and spiritual hindrances seek to prevent our lights from shining as intended.

Perhaps the greatest barrier we face is the pressure placed on believers to perform that which is reserved only for God. We have been told that unless we witness to enough people, we are not representing the light of the world. Unfortunately, this focus has reduced Jesus's statement to specific actions that are often imposed on us by spiritual leaders while neglecting the more important element of spiritual identity. I want every believer to shine bright for the world to see; however, many well-meaning people are made to feel guilty for not doing enough. Others work themselves into a lather trying to conduct evangelism efforts that do not produce fruit. The art of marketing Jesus is not about trying harder to become the light of the world. If we fall into this dangerous trap, we will find ourselves far less effective at attracting others to Jesus.

Many people believe that human behavior is the primary factor that determines spiritual identity. We often feel strongly motivated to achieve for God. However, we must step back and consider the factual nature of the statement "You are the light of the world." Notice that Jesus did not say you *should be* the light of the world. Nor did He say that you *could be* the light of the world with enough effort. On the contrary, Jesus declared without any reservations that *you are* the light of the world. Those who have accepted Jesus as their personal Savior are the light of the world because the Holy Spirit lives inside every believer. Therefore, we must first learn to walk with a greater sense of awareness that we are the light of the world before we take any steps to change the world.

I lived in a foster home for several years until I was adopted. I still remember the first day I was taken away from my foster home to meet my new family. I was playing with some toy army men on the front steps of the house when the social worker arrived in a shiny brown sedan. As she spoke with my foster parents, I got this sinking feeling in my stomach that something wasn't right. The woman glanced in my direction several times and, after a few minutes, asked me to get into the car. Being too young to fully understand the reason for being taken away, I used every ounce of my three-year-old strength to prevent the social worker from putting me in the car. However, no amount of kicking and screaming could stop the inevitable.

After driving down country roads for what seemed an eternity, we finally turned onto a long gravel driveway. As we approached the large brown house at the end of the driveway, we were met by eight people standing in two rows of four. Each person introduced themselves to me in sequential order. Although they were friendly and wanted me to feel welcomed, I refused to say anything in return. Amazingly, many of the details from that day are vivid in my mind. My oldest brother was wearing a Micky Mouse T-shirt, and about fifteen puppies were running around in the side yard. Admittedly, I spent many years of my life thinking about how my transition into the family impacted my world. However, as I grew older, I began to reflect on how God might have orchestrated these events to impact the others in the family.

I am convinced that God had a special purpose for my adoption that was far more significant than merely placing me in a loving home. It's true that I needed a good family to raise me and provide support throughout my life. However, in addition to being the only adopted person in the bunch, I was also the only person with a ministry calling on my life. It didn't matter to me what the others may have believed about Jesus; I was going to follow Him even if that meant traveling the path alone. The fact that I came into the home from the outside and developed an unwavering faith in Jesus, which was not the product of my family's influence, speaks volumes about the sovereign hand of God. I did not have to engage in any specific actions to point my family to Jesus because my presence alone produced at least some measure of spiritual light.

We must not underestimate the power of what God has placed within us. People can sense that we carry spiritual light on our lives without any effort on our part. As we take our kids to school in the morning, drive through the local coffee shop, and arrive at our places of work every day, we carry with us the full radiance of God's presence. We often place too much emphasis on the physical world and fail to see what is happening behind the scenes in the spiritual realm. However, if we believe the Holy Spirit lives within every believer, we must know that our presence alone changes the environment wherever we go. This does not happen because we are trying to create light; it's because we are light.

There was nothing impressive about my spiritual prowess while growing up. On the contrary, my family has seen my failures, shortcomings, and insecurities up close and personal. However, any life that has been touched by the hand of Jesus will create an expression of light despite our inadequacies. For example, one of my brothers told me that although he wasn't sure if God existed at the time, he sensed in his heart that my entrance into the family was divinely orchestrated. On another occasion, a different sibling told me that he was beginning to believe that God might exist after listening to his younger olive-skinned brother's sermons on audio cassette tape. In other words, I was sent to the family as a press release written from heaven to demonstrate that Jesus is real. The message that God wanted to communicate did not require any words out of my mouth because it was solely the work of the Holy Spirit.

When to Speak

Although we are the light of the world without saying one word, there are times when God wants us to speak. However, we must learn to speak only when the Holy Spirit opens the door; otherwise, we will inevitably get in the way. As my faith in Jesus grew stronger, I developed an unhealthy burden to get the other people in my family saved, which resulted in several unskilled attempts at sharing my faith. Many times I felt the need to defend my faith but did not have the internal character to operate in love. I learned that forcing the issue with people will always create more harm than good. Therefore, we must learn to wait for God to open doors and recognize the opportunities He creates to share our faith.

I once had breakfast with a colleague while attending a business conference in California. It was obvious that my colleague knew I was a Christian before we met because he randomly started asking questions about my faith. He was not shy about asking tough questions and often pushed back at my responses, which created a more dynamic conversation. After about ninety minutes, we were informed that the woman sitting next to us had paid our bill. As we leaned over to thank her for her generosity, she stood up with tears in her eyes. "I just became a Christian a few weeks ago and needed to hear these answers." It was clear she wanted to say more, but her words were interrupted by a full-blown "ugly cry" that caused her to quickly leave the restaurant to avoid embarrassment. The moment was so powerful that not even my skeptical business colleague could deny that the scenario must have been divinely orchestrated from heaven.

I did not plan to talk about Jesus with my colleague that day. I certainly had no idea a woman was sitting at the adjacent table, listening to our conversation; however, this is exactly how the art of marketing Jesus works. As we remove every religious barrier and spiritual hindrance that gets in the way, we see that we are the light of the world only because Jesus lives within us. We don't need to work harder to create spiritual light, and we certainly don't need to force the issue regarding sharing our faith. We are merely vessels who have been taken out of the darkness and placed into the light. The apostle Paul reminds us that God is the only One who can cause spiritual growth. "So neither the one who plants nor the one who waters is anything, but only God, who makes things grow" (1 Corinthians 3:7).

There was a time when we were just like the demoniac living among the tombs. We had no ability to rescue ourselves out of the dominion of darkness. We had no light within ourselves to give to other people. However, Jesus traveled across the sea to meet us right where we were and changed our lives forever. He took us out of the darkness and filled us with the glorious light of God. We don't need to try harder to become the light of the world or put unnecessary pressure on ourselves to perform because God has turned every believer into a living press release. If your light has been stuck underneath the bushels of religion, performance, and spiritual bondage, continue reading this book and you will learn how to set your light back on the lampstand of spiritual freedom for everyone to see.

Chapter 2

ATTRACTION MARKETING

Stopping advertising to save money is like stopping your watch

to save time.

HENRY FORD[4]

THE EXPLOSION OF TECHNOLOGY in recent years has resulted in a new form of marketing that took the business world and modern society by storm. Marketers generally refer to this approach as attraction marketing, which represents an alternative form of advertising that draws target audiences through the creation of digital content, such as blogs, videos, infographics, ebooks, white papers, podcasts, and more. Search engine optimization, social media, and other strategies are used within attraction marketing to draw people to the brand. As you can imagine, the effectiveness of attraction marketing is based largely on the quality of the digital content that is produced. It's why marketers spend considerable time researching the needs and tendencies of their target audiences so they might become more skilled at creating content that attracts the right people.

For example, my wife has a particular interest in learning about health and nutrition concepts that help people achieve their fitness goals. As a result, she listens to several podcasts that offer valuable insights on those subjects. My two young boys, on the other hand, are mesmerized by YouTube channels that focus on video games and toys. Many of these channels have hundreds of thousands, and in some cases millions, of subscribers. *Ryan's World* is one of the most popular YouTube channels made for kids that focuses on unpacking and demoing new toys. In just six years, the channel grew from zero followers to over twenty-seven million subscribers. The content creators even started their line of proprietary toys that are sold in several major retail stores, all through the power of attraction marketing.

This novel marketing approach has proven itself superior in many ways over the alternative and more traditional form of marketing, appropriately referred to as disruption marketing. Disruption marketing represents an entirely different methodology because it seeks to capture new customers through the process of interruption. By strategically placing advertisements, such as billboards and television commercials, in the places where people live, work, and play, companies use the power of repetition to create memorable impressions in the mind of consumers. However, the beauty of attraction marketing is that consumers can choose to digest content that adds value to their lives, whereas disruption marketing is essentially forced upon the masses. Let's be honest, did anybody choose to memorize the words to the well-known jingle *Plop, plop, fizz, fizz, oh what a relief it is*? It's for this reason, brands that incorporate attraction marketing concepts are often perceived by their audiences as more credible experts.

Open-Air Preaching

Years ago, the Lord impressed upon my heart to do the unthinkable. He asked me to conduct open-air dialogues with students on the University of Washington campus while capturing the interactions on film. If that proposition sounds a bit outrageous to you, just imagine how I felt. Open-air dialogues on campus

... really, God? However, I have learned over the years that God-inspired assignments are always bigger than what we can handle on our own. I did not have the courage within myself to conduct open-air dialogues, but I sensed in my heart that the opportunity represented a defining moment in my life. Would I cave under the fear of stepping outside my comfort zone, or would I choose to obey God's instructions? Thankfully, by the grace of God, I chose the latter.

After working out the details with the university to make sure my efforts were aboveboard, I marched onto campus with a videographer. We were required to conduct the open-air sessions on the section of campus known as Red Square, which attracts the most foot traffic. After pacing for about an hour and watching hundreds of students pass by, I, terrified half to death, finally started speaking. You heard that right. I stood on the busiest part of campus and preached to the students. The University of Washington is one of the most secular higher education institutions in the United States. Only God could get me to do something this crazy.

I continued to visit the campus multiple times per month, which resulted in many hours of preaching. At first, I did not see the results I was expecting. Because of the high volume of foot traffic on campus, my heart was set on catching a large number of "fish." The truth is, my efforts felt more like casting a single fishing line into a small stream. I was pleased to see a few students respond to the gospel, but most of the people seemed disinterested. Over time, the lack of results began to wear me down. When you spend days preaching to nameless people without getting the hoped-for results, it's easy to question the fruit of your labor. Why did God even bother?

As time went on, I discovered that some tactics worked better than others. Specifically, when a student stopped to ask questions about Jesus, the interactions took on a whole new meaning. Based on the response I received in those moments, it was clear the students were more interested in listening to the dialogues than hearing me preach, and I sensed that the Holy Spirit was divinely orchestrating those interactions. Finally, after many hours of trial and error, I changed my approach. The new strategy was simple. Instead of doing all the talking, I offered a more obvious way for students to ask questions. I created an A-board sign with a huge question mark at the center. Beneath the question mark, the sign read, "Ask your toughest questions about God, Jesus, Christianity, and the Bible." I placed the sign at the center of the location where I was speaking and set up a microphone that faced directly away from me. The setting was obvious. Step up to the microphone and ask your toughest questions about Jesus, but don't forget to smile—you're on camera!

To my surprise, the new strategy was far more effective. From that day forward, I spent about ten minutes speaking to the crowds to get the ball rolling but then gave the remainder of the time to students who wanted to ask questions. It goes without saying that when Jesus is discussed in a public forum, it will always attract a few knuckleheads who want to cause problems. However, despite the occasional troublemaker, I was pleased to discover that most of the students asked genuine questions. The days of laboring through extended hours of open-air preaching were replaced with meaningful dialogues that focused on the person of Jesus. I stumbled across the same attraction marketing concepts that are commonly used in the business world, only I was in the business of attracting people to Jesus.

The benefits of changing my approach to the attraction model cannot be overstated. For starters, my energy was no longer focused on people with no interest in learning about Jesus. Instead, I provided a content-based spiritual service that relied on the Holy Spirit to lead people to the microphone, not to mention the many students who often gathered around to hear the dialogues. The gospel was still being communicated, but I would argue in a more effective way for the intended audience. The new approach took the focus away from me and placed it on the needs of the students. Most important, I was in a better position to respect the dignity of the people in a way that expressed God's love more effectively.

The spiritual rewards I experienced were deeply enriching. It was a blessing to watch certain students quietly listen to the dialogues for hours and then come back the next day to hear more. I knew that God was working in their hearts. I also had the opportunity to become friends with a few hard-core atheists whom I never would have known otherwise. Some of the students asked for prayer and privately sought out spiritual guidance. I even had a Muslim person openly honor me in front of the crowd, stating that I was doing a good thing by helping people learn more about Jesus. In short, I did my best to treat the students with respect, and my approach may have earned their respect in return. It was through the power of attraction, not disruption, that produced better results.

Don't forget, we also filmed the interactions. I was able to package hours of dialogue into short question-oriented video clips. The videos provided the perfect digital asset to extend the ministry into an online attraction model that reached far beyond the campus. I posted the videos online and shared them on social media. Some of the students used the videos to conduct Bible studies and initiate private conversations with their friends. I was invited to speak about Jesus at other schools, including Pepperdine University, which gave me the opportunity to introduce Jesus to thousands of people. I was even interviewed by a local radio station and featured in a television news story halfway across the country. I do not believe these results would have been possible had I not changed my strategy to an attraction-based model.

Marketing Gold

We were created to enjoy a love relationship with our Creator, but every love relationship must be founded on mutual choice. Otherwise, the possibility of a genuine relationship does not exist. Imagine if you were forced to become a Christian, or that you were programmed to choose Christ. It's clear that in either case, the relationship would not be genuine because you would not have been given a free choice. Therefore, the only acceptable approach to forming a love relationship that preserves the dignity of humanity is through the power of attraction. It's for this reason God does not manipulate, coerce, or deceive people into a relationship; rather, He works behind the scenes to draw people with His love. The Lord told Israel, "I have loved you with an everlasting love; I have drawn you with unfailing kindness" (Jeremiah 31:3).

God has already chosen you. His love was put on display two thousand years ago with the death of Jesus on the cross. Jesus said, "Greater love has no one than this: to lay down one's life for one's friends" (John 15:13). However, despite the incredible expression of love on the cross, God is not sitting around hoping that we stumble across a Billy Graham crusade on television and get saved. Instead, He is actively working to divinely persuade people to put their trust in Christ. He goes out of His way to gently tug at our hearts and send personal love letters when we need them the most. He is doing everything possible behind the scenes to get our attention. As a result, when someone chooses to put their trust in Jesus, it has absolutely nothing to do with blind faith; rather, the decision is based on the intimate work that God has done in the human heart.

God's plan to attract people originates from the Father's passionate love for humanity—which is why Jesus was sent to die on the cross. Since Jesus represents the only way a person can be saved, He also represents the centerpiece of the attraction model. Ultimately, I am not interested in helping people find Christianity or to put their faith in the church. These are mere entities that do not have the power to save and can be manipulated by people to serve their own purposes. At the end of the day, the art of marketing Jesus is about pointing people to the Son of God so they might receive eternal life. Jesus said it this way, "I am the gate; whoever enters through me will be saved" (John 10:9).

Many belief systems in the world seek to capture our attention. Some people have put their faith in science, naturalism, or materialism. Others believe that Muhammad points the way to God. Ultimately, we have all chosen to believe in something. However, we must keep in mind that no matter which option we choose, we are trusting that option with our very lives. In a world of competing alternatives, we can be certain that because Jesus is God, there is no other reliable worldview. Jesus is the only person who lived a sinless life, taught amazing ethical teachings, loved even His most brutal enemies, and rose from the dead. As believers, we have the only solution that can satisfy the deepest needs of humanity. It's why Jesus can be described as nothing less than pure marketing gold. When the authentic Jesus is put on display for the world to see, He will draw all people to Himself. "And I, when I am lifted up from the earth, will draw all people to myself" (John 12:32).

The ministry of the Holy Spirit is ultimately responsible for leading people to Jesus and causing them to be saved. However, we must not overlook the role that believers play in the attraction marketing strategy. Jesus is the gate that leads to salvation, but believers have the awesome privilege of helping people find the gate. However, the way God uses ordinary people to attract others to Jesus is far more profound than speaking to students on campus. As we discussed in the previous chapter, every believer represents the living embodiment of spiritual light, but some may feel they are too spiritually broken to shine light. Despite how you may feel today, it's a wonder to behold that God uses the limitations of finite humanity, which is often seen in our greatest weaknesses, failures, and pain, to showcase the eternal glory of God.

Why Did This Happen?

As a child, I often wondered why I was separated from my family at birth. I didn't know anybody else who was adopted. It seemed that all the other kids had a normal experience growing up. I needed to understand why this happened to me. My question was not related to the logistical reasons that created my situation. Instead, I was asking a philosophical question that was meant to reconcile the reality of suffering with the existence of a loving God. Nobody is exempt from painful experiences in life, but it's what we believe about our pain that has lasting implications. If the atheistic worldview is the truth, then my sufferings were void of any meaning. The logical ramification of atheism is that everything happens by accident, including our very existence, which means that I was simply less fortunate than others. However, if there is a loving God who cares deeply about humanity, which is exactly what Jesus communicated to the world, then my sufferings carried significant spiritual meaning.

In the year 2000, I began a search for my biological mother, which led me to request the adoption paperwork from the agency that handled my case. When the paperwork arrived, I noticed that a permanent ink marker was used to black out large portions of the information. Curious, I held the papers over a light, which allowed me to read every word. Unfortunately, what I discovered was that my biological mother suffered from chronic mental illness. Due to no fault of her own, she refused to hold me immediately after my birth and exhibited other troubling behaviors related to her illness. Despite the upsetting nature of the details, I continued to hold the paper over the light and read everything that was hidden beneath the black ink. When it comes to the deep wounds in our souls, we simply cannot keep the truth hidden forever.

The revelations about my mother would have been difficult enough on their own; however, they only worked to bolster the feeling that I was destined to share the same outcome in life. Coincidentally, the family who adopted me also experienced the devastating impacts of mental illness. Therefore, I was already traumatized having lived under similar circumstances. My heart breaks for those who struggle with mental illness. I can't imagine the pain that one must go through suffering from schizophrenia and other diseases. However, I can best relate to those who have experienced severe trauma having witnessed their loved ones suffer from mental illness. It can be very scary and confusing growing up in these environments. Nobody comes out unaffected.

In my case, the trauma I experienced developed into post-traumatic stress disorder (PTSD). Starting in my early twenties, I began to have flashbacks related to the frightening events I saw growing up. The flashbacks were accompanied by panic attacks and severe bouts of anxiety. On many occasions, I believed I was going crazy and could not escape the fear that my life was on the brink of ruin. The one saving grace that kept me going was knowing that I was not biologically related to my family. The problem of mental illness is often closely related to biological factors, so in that sense, it was comforting to know that I was not related. However, after learning about my biological mother, that small amount of comfort was swept away. It felt like my worst nightmare was inevitable.

The height of my anxiety and panic attacks lasted for over fifteen years. During that time, I tried to mask the pain by stuffing myself with food. When you're living with chronic fear and anxiety, you don't think about your lifestyle choices from a logical standpoint. You just want to escape the pain. I went from being a thin and relatively athletic person in high school to almost three hundred pounds during my mid-twenties. My poor eating habits eventually developed into type 2 diabetes. Fortunately, I have been able to manage the diabetes through diet and exercise alone. However, during the many years I was learning how to manage PTSD, I often struggled to believe that I would ever feel normal again.

I would be remiss to ignore the fallacy that assumes people with mental health issues don't have enough faith. This notion that exists within many Christian circles could not be further from the truth. Mental health disease is often related to a combination of environmental and biological factors. To be clear, my struggles did not come from a lack of faith; rather, it was my faith that paved the way to healing. As it happened, I finally reached the point where I could not take the pain any longer. While driving in my car one day, I began to earnestly cry out to the Lord for help. After a few minutes of praying for a way out of my situation, I turned on the radio to listen to music. Instantly, when I pushed the start button on the radio, an advertisement began from an organization that helps people overcome anxiety and panic attacks. There was no question in my mind that God had miraculously responded to my prayer. I called the phone number for help.

Although my recovery took place over several years, from that moment forward, I never lost faith that God would restore me completely. When given the opportunity to speak at church, I often encouraged people to press toward their promised land. I firmly believe that every believer has been given the promises of victory and divine purpose. However, giants that want to occupy our blessings will always seek to keep us from entering the land that belongs to us. You might be facing the giant of anxiety, depression, or addiction, but you must keep believing that sustainable victory belongs to you. You must accept that what you are going through today is part of an amazing testimony that will give God the most amount of glory in your life.

Today, I have learned how to manage the mental health issues that severely plagued my life for so many years. It was only through the process of learning how to secure my victory in the Lord that helps me to stay free today. When anxiety and panic try to rear their ugly heads again, I have already developed the spiritual skills to hold my ground and trust that God will see me through. I have put into practice the teachings from the apostle Paul, including "We demolish arguments and every pretension that sets itself up against the knowledge of God, and we take captive every thought to make it obedient to Christ" (2 Corinthians

10:5). I have learned how to manage these giants in partnership with God and lean into the words of Paul when things are tough: "I can do all this through him who gives me strength" (Philippians 4:13).

One day when I was starting to get better from the mental health issues, I asked God, "What have You done for me that I never realized was You?" Before I could even finish the question, the Holy Spirit interrupted me with the most unexpected response: *I put you in the Wachter family!* I never realized the extent to which God had orchestrated my life, but His response challenged me to see my circumstances through a different lens. Why did this happen to me? I can tell you that despite the many challenges I have experienced throughout my life, I would not change a single thing. It was only through the pain, suffering, and setbacks that paved the way for God to get the most amount of glory in my life. I have made peace with my sufferings, knowing that God works all things together for good.

My point in sharing this with you is to underscore that when we see the world through the lens of faith, we discover that God is in the process of using every painful experience to shine light into the world. We must not believe that attracting people to Jesus comes from our own strengths, talents, or human efforts. On the contrary, the light of the world is most clearly seen through our struggles, weaknesses, and limitations. If you feel that you are too broken or unqualified to shine light, I have good news for you. When it comes to attracting people to Jesus, God makes a point to use the foolish things of the world to confound the wise, and the weak things of the world to confound the strong. Let these words fill your heart with a great sense of purpose as it relates to your struggles. The reason you are having so much trouble is that God is getting ready to shine light through your life.

One day Jesus saw a man who was blind from birth, which prompted His disciples to ask a very philosophical question, "Rabbi, who sinned, this man or his parents, that he was born blind?" (John 9:2). This question shows the real reason we often struggle to understand our pain. Like the disciples, we tend to see the world through a natural lens and conclude that our painful experiences are limited to natural explanations. We might conclude that we have suffered because someone else made a mistake or because we are simply unlucky. As a result, we fail to see the deeper spiritual implications related to our troubles. Jesus responded to the disciples, "Neither this man nor his parents sinned, but this happened so that the works of God might be displayed in him" (John 9:3).

In this response, Jesus provided the answer to our deepest question associated with pain and suffering: Why did this happen to me? Although God does not cause every painful experience, like the blind man, all things have been permitted so that the works of God might be displayed in us. When the former demoniac was sent back to his people, the effectiveness of his ministry was not based on his abilities; rather, it was based on what God had done through his weaknesses. In the same way, we must trust that God has the power to work all things together for good and that our limitations represent the greatest opportunity for light to shine. When we see the world through the lens of faith, we understand that the power of Christ rests upon us because we are limited. We are the light of the world for this reason alone.

Authentic Marketing

In the world of marketing, it's difficult to find success when the message conveyed to the public is not authentic. People can smell phoniness and are repulsed when a company is not honest in its marketing campaigns. Have you ever received a letter that is formatted like an official invoice, only to find out that it's really a promotion from a mortgage company wanting you to refinance? If you're anything like me, you get annoyed that someone would even try to solicit your business that way. Those letters belong in the trashcan because they are not authentic. When attracting people to Jesus, we must understand that until we're willing to be genuine, our lights will not shine brightly.

After Jesus healed the blind man, the people who formerly saw him begging could not believe their eyes. Many were convinced that he only looked like the person who was blind. Finally, he spoke up for himself and insisted, "I am the man." The blind man was not willing to hide in the corner and pretend that he was never blind. On the contrary, he was quite emphatic about his past condition because he understood that transparency was the only way for the people to understand that a miracle truly happened. In the same way, we must not hide in the corner and pretend that we were never healed from a variety of past conditions or act like we have it all together today. Otherwise, we are only dimming our lights behind the veil of pride. People need to hear our stories and receive encouragement that God can work in their lives too.

Unfortunately, many well-meaning believers overly focus on the perfection of God and fail to recognize the human side of following Jesus. It's for this reason divorced individuals often do not feel comfortable attending church. Others avoid faith communities altogether because they have been given a false perception that everyone is living the perfect life. If we lose sight of our past conditions and fail to present ourselves as genuine, we are only creating an environment where broken people believe they don't belong. We must not allow ourselves to become plastic believers, always putting on a smile and saying the right words but never telling anybody our real stories. Instead, we must stand in faith and declare our victory in the Lord while being genuine about our weaknesses and limitations.

The writers of the Gospels did not paint a rosy picture about what happened in the first century. They documented every relevant detail, including the good, the bad, and the ugly, which has the effect of giving the Gospels greater credibility. The writers recorded the victory that Jesus secured by rising from the dead without glossing over the messy things that happened on the way to the cross. Have we forgotten that hundreds of people stopped following Jesus because they didn't understand His teachings? Or that Judas, one of the twelve disciples, betrayed the Messiah with a kiss for a few silver coins? Should we overlook the fact that Peter denied knowing Jesus? Or that due to enormous stress, Jesus was human enough to sweat drops of blood? We must understand the power of the gospel is most clearly seen when God works through the limitations of finite humanity.

I'll be the first to admit that it's not easy to acknowledge our real stories. Perhaps you went through a painful divorce, recovered from an addiction, or were fired from your job. Or like me, maybe you've struggled with mental health issues. We can take courage in knowing that despite the setbacks we've experienced in life, we're always in good company when we choose to be genuine. You might be surprised to learn that even the famous prophet Elijah struggled with his mental health. The same powerful man who called fire down from heaven and killed hundreds of false prophets with the sword also became so disillusioned that he quit the ministry, fell into a deep depression, and became suicidal. How many people today struggle in the same way but feel uncomfortable telling their stories in church because we have not understood the value of authenticity? I am convinced that when we see the limitations of our heroes in the faith, we better understand that God can use anybody to accomplish great things.

One of the hallmarks of the modern church in recent years has been the explosion of incredible worship music. Some may not agree, but I am pleased when worship teams take their music on the road and sell out large arenas. However, what would happen if we changed the lyrics in their songs to some of the lamenting words found in the psalms? Imagine putting these words to a contemporary melody, "My soul is in deep anguish. How long, Lord, how long?" (Psalm 6:3). Here's another lyric to get the party started, "Why, Lord, do you stand far off? Why do you hide yourself in times of trouble?" (Psalm 10:1). I'm being facetious, of course, but I am also convinced that it's through the honesty of the psalmists that we gain deeper insights into how God uses the limitations of humanity to shine light into the world. It's comforting to know that King David, the man who took down Goliath with a sling, at times felt like he couldn't make it another day. If the psalmists had not been willing to share their genuine stories, we would not know the depths from which they were delivered, nor would we be the recipients of their encouragement today.

Jesus Will Find You

As you continue the journey through the art of marketing Jesus, I invite you to embrace your painful experiences as the greatest opportunity for God to shine light through your life. However, like the blind man, you must be willing to tell your real story. That doesn't mean you should go around telling everyone about your problems, but it does mean that if you are too embarrassed to be genuine, your light will stay hidden. However, I must tell you that in the process of sharing what Jesus has done in your life, not everyone will accept what you have to say. Many people prefer to walk in darkness, and they get upset when the light of truth shines in the world. Therefore, you must be willing to take a stand and not allow yourself to shrink back from telling people about Jesus.

After the blind man was healed, the religious leaders summoned him to tell his story. Like many people today, the leaders did not want to hear the truth because they had their minds made up about Jesus. Therefore, they proceeded to insult him for being genuine. Finally, the religious leaders threw him out of the temple because the man would not change his story. In the same way, some people will choose to insult, berate, and even throw you out of their lives for believing in Jesus. You may have to say goodbye to people you have known for many years. However, it's comforting to know that after the man was thrown out of the temple, Jesus went out of His way to find him and lead him to salvation. It's painful when we are rejected and pushed away simply for believing in Jesus. But we can take courage in knowing that although we have been rejected by some people, Jesus has made certain that we have been received by Him.

Chapter 3

BRAND IMAGE

Your brand is what other people say about you
when you're not in the room.

JEFF BEZOS[5]

I WALKED DOWN THE aisle of the local grocery store in search of my first deodorant stick. I never had to think about this type of product before, but my reputation heading into junior high was contingent on having good hygiene. The options seemed endless, but two brands stood out to me for completely different reasons. In a matter of seconds, I was able to conclude that Speed Stick was the right choice for me and that Old Spice was the wrong choice. That was the moment I became a loyal Speed Stick customer.

I didn't think about the psychology of my purchasing behavior at the time. Looking back, however, it's clear that I didn't care about the quality of the product—it was the branding that mattered most to me. For reasons I could not have explained then, Speed Stick just felt like the right option. The name, logo, and colors resonated with me. Old Spice, on the other hand . . . well, not so much. That brand seemed tired and out-of-touch. I remember thinking that Old Spice was the product for old people and that I would never purchase it, even when I was old.

This sentiment stayed with me through high school and well beyond my college years. I tried other products that came on the scene, such as Axe, which seemed more relevant, but no way was I was going to spend money on Old Spice. I wasn't alone either. Old Spice product sales were going down the drain, and the company was rapidly losing market share to other brands. The executives knew that a significant change was needed, so they hired a marketing agency called Wieden+Kennedy to turn things around.

The Old Spice brand had grown outdated, but its name was still highly recognizable, which provided enough brand equity to position the company for a most impressive comeback. The change started with a rebrand of their underperforming scent called Glacial Falls. They changed the name to Swagger and rolled out a spunky advertising and social media campaign that produced a 400 percent increase in sales for just that product. A couple of years later, Old Spice continued the turnaround with the Smell Like a Man, Man campaign that was designed to rejuvenate their line of scented body washes. And, man, did it work!

Wieden+Kennedy released a case study that referred to the Old Spice campaign as "the fastest-growing and most popular interactive campaign in history."[6] According to another study, more people watched the campaign videos in twenty-four hours than watched Obama's presidential victory speech. The campaign garnered forty million video views in one week, and social media impressions were approximately 1.4 billion.[7] As a result of the campaign, not only did product sales skyrocket but also, more important, Old Spice changed its reputation from an outdated brand to the cool brand everyone loved. Even I made the switch to Old Spice and have been using their products since 2008.

In the world of business, perhaps nothing is more important than branding. Branding is the art and science that defines and articulates the identity of an organization to the world. Many elements go into making that happen, including a company name, logo, identity, tagline, story, personality, values, and more. The methodologies and strategies behind creating these elements might appear simple to the naked eye, but they require a sophisticated level of expertise and long-term commitment to develop a brand that resonates with its target audience.

Marketers have every intention of using these strategies to differentiate a company from its competition and create brand loyalty. The methodologies are meant to shape what the general public believes about the brand. However, an important marketing term called *brand image* measures how brands are perceived in real life. Make no mistake, how a brand wishes to be perceived does not always match how the market perceives it. Therefore, a company must always be aware of the impression it makes on the public and have its finger on the pulse of what people think about the brand.

It helps to think of brand image the same way you think about a person. The Old Spice case study shows that customers did not want to associate with a boring personality. Instead, they preferred a brand that is fun, cool, and has a great sense of humor. Old Spice needed to elevate its status from being identified as the uninteresting person with no friends to the hilarious person everyone loves to be around. The strategy behind the advertising campaign gave the brand a personality makeover that captured the imagination of its target audience and produced wildly successful results practically overnight. In short, the brand image of the company was elevated in the mind of consumers.

In the same way, we must take an honest look at how the Christian faith is perceived by the public. Are believers known for having the same qualities that attracted people to Jesus in the first century, or are we better known for having judgmental attitudes? Are we spreading a message of good news, or has the message been corroded with doom-and-gloom and religious dogma? Are we known for being genuine people in touch with our shortcomings, or have we become synonymous with the word *hypocrisy*?

We must explore these questions to determine if we are accurately representing the gospel brand to the world. If we evaluate our brand image and don't like the results, we must learn to better define the gospel from inside the Christian ranks. Only then can we make the necessary changes to improve public perception on the outside. If done correctly, this process will not compromise the integrity of our faith. On the contrary, it will work to clarify the true meaning of the gospel and attract people to Jesus.

Jesus Versus Pharisees

When Jesus walked the earth, a religious group called the Pharisees had spiritual influence over many Jewish people. The Pharisees called for strict adherence to God's written law and their own add-on laws no matter the cost. This may have seemed like a noble pursuit at the time, but the leaders of the group did not have an accurate understanding of God. As a result, their faulty ideology transformed them into religious charlatans.

Jesus did not mince words when expressing displeasure toward the Pharisees. He called them hypocrites, blind guides, whitewashed tombs, and snakes! Jesus exposed that these religious leaders put heavy rules on others while not keeping the same rules themselves. He called out their hypocrisy in wanting to look holy in public places, even though they were riddled with spiritual pride on the inside. He warned that the religious leaders were preventing people from entering heaven. In short, the Pharisees represented the antithesis of the grace and truth that Jesus embodied. As a result, they have become synonymous with the worst kind of religious hypocrisy.

One of the most prominent researchers on topics of faith and Christianity, the Barna Group, conducted a study to measure the extent to which believers in modern society possess the attitudes and actions of Jesus versus the attitudes and actions of the Pharisees. The study involved a series of questions and categories that were used to distinguish Jesus qualities from Pharisee qualities. The participants were asked to rank the qualities, which then allowed the researchers to aggregate the results and place each study participant into one of four quadrants:

- Christ-like in action and attitude
- Christ-like in action, but not in attitude
- Christ-like in attitude, but not in action
- Christ-like in neither

The results showed that 51 percent of "self-identified Christians in the United States are characterized by having the attitudes and actions researchers identified as Pharisaical."[8] These people fell into the quadrant *Christ-like in neither* regarding their actions and attitudes. Only 14 percent of self-identified Christians fell into the quadrant *Christ-like in action and attitude*. The implications of the data suggest that most believers in modern society have adopted attitudes and behaviors that are aligned more with the Pharisees than with Christ. It should go without saying that these results do not bode well for creating a brand image that attracts people to Jesus.

Before we consider how to restore the brand image of the gospel, we must first identify the root cause of the problem. At its core, the Pharisees were known for their self-righteous, judgmental, and heartless actions because they embraced a deep-rooted belief system that was inherently flawed. Instead of seeing God as a gracious and merciful Father, they believed in a demanding rule-enforcer whose primary interest was keeping people in line. It was their skewed mind-set that rendered them incompatible with the grace and truth that Jesus personified.

One day I was at the church office putting together a message for the service later that evening. The campus was closed at that time, so I was alarmed to see a stranger walking down the hallway. The man had a certain look in his eye that let me know he came with an agenda. Before I had a chance to ask how I could help, the stranger proceeded to ask a series of probing questions about the church and our theology. After a couple of minutes of trying to reason with the man, and getting nowhere in the process, I asked him a simple question. "Who is your pastor?" I have learned over the years that people who think like a Pharisee often verbally challenge spiritual leaders, but they rarely invite spiritual leaders to speak into their own lives.

"Jesus Christ is my pastor," he quipped. In other words, the man was a rogue agent for Jesus.

What occurred next can be described as the classic example of what happens when you engage with someone who thinks like a Pharisee. The man insisted that we must get back to a rules-based way of relating to God. He expressed strong dissatisfaction with churches that worship on Sunday instead of Saturday. He also made clear that anyone who does not agree with his religious views is not part of the "true" church. I do not do well with unfruitful conversations, so I asked the man to leave the building. On his way out the door, he revealed the true colors of what thinking like a Pharisee does to people. As a last-ditch effort, he shouted, "I shake the dust off my feet! You are going straight to hell!" Coincidentally, the message I was preparing for later that evening was about learning how to stand against lies from Satan.

The extent to which a person thinks like a Pharisee, that person will act like a Pharisee. Many people in modern society are reading books, researching online articles, and listening to teachers with strong Pharisaical influences. Jesus told us what happens when we entertain concepts that are not based on truth: "The eye is the lamp of the body. If your eyes are healthy, your whole body will be full of light. But if your eyes are unhealthy, your whole body will be full of darkness. If then the light within you is darkness, how great is that darkness!" (Matthew 6:22–23). In other words, if we invite Pharisaical ideas into our lives, our souls will be captivated by the same darkness that shaped the Pharisees. As a result, we begin to see the world through the lens of a rule-enforcer and place our lights under the basket of religion.

Self-Righteous, Judgmental, and Heartless

We can start the process of restoring the brand image of the gospel by creating awareness of how thinking like a Pharisee manifests into behaviors. It helps to separate the behaviors into three general categories: *self-righteous*, *judgmental*, and *heartless*. Each of these categories produces a domino effect in how they shape the actions of people. First, the Pharisees were *self-righteous* as revealed in the parable of the Pharisee and the tax collector. Second, the Pharisees were *judgmental* in their effort to chastise Jesus for associating with disreputable people. Third, the Pharisees were *heartless* in their desire to throw stones at the woman caught in adultery.

Self-Righteous: The Gateway Drug

In the same way that marijuana is the gateway drug to more dangerous drug use, inviting self-righteous thinking into our lives is the first step to becoming a full-blown Pharisee. Self-righteous people seek to establish their right standing with God based on human performance. This idea runs contrary to the very essence of the gospel. If people can achieve righteousness based on their performance, Jesus's death on the cross and His subsequent resurrection were in vain.

Paul, who was once a prominent Pharisee himself, shared his concern for those trapped in this ideology. "For I can testify about them that they are zealous for God, but their zeal is not based on knowledge. Since they did not know the righteousness of God and sought to *establish their own*, they did not submit to God's righteousness" (Romans 10:2–3). Many people today have a similar zeal for God, as the Pharisees did in the first century, but they lack the biblical understanding of righteousness. Therefore, they get caught in the trap of trusting in their spiritual performance to maintain their right standing with God.

In the context of the modern church, we have been conditioned to believe that certain human activities, such as prayer, Bible reading, church attendance, home schooling, serving people, and even avoiding sinful actions factor into what makes a person righteous. Some have pushed this agenda to the point that many well-meaning believers don't feel righteous until they complete enough tasks from their religious checklist. We must draw a clear line in the sand and recognize that adherence to programs, disciplines, and behaviors—including any attempt to maintain God's written laws—will never make a person righteous before God.

Scripture is clear that those who have been rescued from spiritual death are made righteous based solely on the performance of Jesus. Paul wrote, "For just as through the disobedience of the one man the many were made sinners, so also through the obedience of the one man the many will be made righteous" (5:19). The disobedience of Adam, the first man God created, produced a ripple effect that contaminated the human condition of every descendent thereafter. As a result, we were all born sinners based on no fault of our own. In the same way, when we trust in Jesus for salvation, we are born righteous based on no good deeds of our own.

People get into trouble when they conflate who is ultimately responsible for their righteousness. The moment we take credit for our right standing with God—or trust in ourselves to stay right with God—we are inhaling the same drug that intoxicated the Pharisees with spiritual pride. When this happens, we will inevitably compare ourselves against others. After all, if human activities can make us right with God, then it makes logical sense to hold in contempt those who are underperforming. Jesus was known for hanging out with all types of disreputable people despite their spiritual performance. As a result, the sinners were drawn to Him. However, those who have given way to self-righteousness have the opposite effect on people.

Have you ever known a person who makes you feel inadequate in their presence? Such individuals seek to maintain a series of rules to feel more in control of their lives, but deep down they struggle with uncertainty, jealousy, and fear. Therefore, as a type of coping mechanism, they become skilled at comparing their best against someone else's worst. What usually follows are nonverbal disapproving signals that repel people like the skunk's scent repels its predators. If we insist on playing the comparison game, we must compare ourselves only against the perfect standard of God. Otherwise, we will look down on those who are lost, struggling, or don't adhere to the same religious checklist.

In the parable of the Pharisee and the tax collector, Jesus revealed the ugly truth behind self-righteousness: "Two men went up to the temple to pray, one a Pharisee and the other a tax collector. The Pharisee stood by himself and prayed: 'God, I thank you that I am not like other people—robbers, evildoers, adulterers—or even like this tax collector. I fast twice a week and give a tenth of all I get'" (Luke 18:10–12). In one fell swoop, the Pharisee managed to score a trifecta concerning self-righteous behaviors. First, he propped himself up above other people. Second, he insulted the tax collector who was also praying in the temple. Third, he bragged about his ability to keep the rules. God is not impressed with our spiritual performance. If we place any confidence in our abilities—as opposed to trusting in Jesus alone for righteousness—we fail to see that even our most valiant efforts are viewed as no better than filthy rags to God.

Jesus revealed that it was the tax collector, not the religious leader, who came away from the prayer justified before God. When the tax collector prayed, he would not even look up to heaven because he knew that his failures were many. "God, have mercy on me, a sinner!" he cried (Luke 18:13). This man did not follow the rules. He had nothing to offer God. However, despite his many failures, the tax collector could look in the mirror and see himself clearly, which drove him, with a broken and contrite heart, to the Lord. Jesus said that it was the humility of the tax collector that allowed him to receive the gift of righteousness.

Much has been said about the virtue of humility, but at its core, humility is nothing more than a willingness to see ourselves from a clear and accurate perspective. Humility sees that living a good life does not make us better than other people. Humility understands that we were created in the image of God and therefore have intrinsic value. Humility does not seek to earn the approval of God because it understands that human effort cannot measure up to His perfect standard. At the end of the day, true humility has learned to rest fully in the finished work of Christ—nothing more, and nothing less.

Judgmental: Fully Intoxicated

Those who are fully intoxicated with spiritual pride will eventually show signs of judgmentalism. Judgmental people feel emboldened to impose stringent demands, harsh criticisms, and moral declarations on other people. At this point in the process, the self-righteous mind-set has created a sense of moral superiority that causes people to dress in black robes so they might function as self-proclaimed spiritual judges in all matters. In a nutshell, judgmental people are far more preoccupied with fighting about what they are against than expressing God's love to others.

Before we go any further on this topic, it's important to underscore how we must approach the issue of moral judgments. I am convinced that believers are not called to be spiritual zombies with no ability to judge between right and wrong. Neither are they called to surrender their sense of moral indignation with respect to evil that exists in the world. On the contrary, believers are called to marinate their spiritual discernment in the love of Christ so that when they encounter actions and behaviors that are morally wrong, they are moved with compassion to help a hurting world. This heart attitude represents the catalyst that brings the ministry of reconciliation, restoration, and hope into the lives of broken people.

Perhaps the most famous statement Jesus ever made — do not judge, or you too will be judged — has been used for centuries to normalize certain behaviors and excuse wrongdoing. However, when we look at the verse in context, we see that such an interpretation is far too simplistic: "Do not judge, or you too will be judged. For in the same way you judge others, you will be judged, and with the measure you use, it will be measured to you" (Matthew 7:1-2). This statement does not prohibit believers from making moral judgments; rather, it offers a strong word of caution that is meant to temper our moral judgments with the same understanding, generosity, and grace we would want to receive under the same circumstances.

Unfortunately, those who think like a Pharisee find it difficult to balance their moral judgments with the compassion of Christ. The fallacy of believing that human effort is responsible for maintaining right standing with God has blinded their eyes from seeing the magnitude of their failures, which, in turn, prevents them from receiving the love of God into their hearts. Where there is an absence of God's experiential love in the human heart, people are far more inclined to treat others harshly or to completely dismiss them altogether.

One day Jesus was invited to a dinner party at the home of a Pharisee. After everyone was reclined at the table, which was customary "seating" in the first century, a woman with an alabaster jar of perfume entered the home. This woman is described in the Bible as having a sinful lifestyle, which means that her questionable behaviors were well-known. Most likely she was a local prostitute—the last person a religious leader in the first century wanted in his home. In what must have been an uncomfortable and somewhat awkward scene, the woman proceeded to kiss the feet of Jesus and clean them with her flowing tears. She then poured the alabaster jar of perfume over His feet.

Simon, the Pharisee who had invited Jesus to his home, was offended that Jesus allowed the woman to express her love in this manner. "If this man were a prophet, he would know who is touching him and what kind of woman she is—that she is a sinner" (Luke 7:39). Notice the dismissive nature of Simon's response. Despite the obvious brokenness and repentance the woman displayed through her tears, the Pharisee could see only a sinner. To make matters worse, he called into question Jesus's ability to make an accurate moral judgment about her lifestyle.

People who think like a Pharisee are far more offended by sinful actions than they are concerned about the people behind the actions. When this happens, they tend to dehumanize others based on selective categories of sin. You may have seen this play out with people who show virtually no concern for those trapped in the cycle of homosexuality or for those who belong to the wrong political party. When we see people as caricatures within a particular category of sin, it has an ever-increasing callusing effect on the human heart. Over time, it becomes much easier to routinely dismiss, criticize, and condemn others that exist outside of our religious paradigms.

Jesus had no problem judging the spiritual condition of the woman. He was fully aware of her checkered past, but He also understood that despite her sinful behaviors, she was still created in the image of God. His moral judgment was not focused on what could be seen on the outside. Instead, He saw the repentant heart of the woman and received her expression of love with open arms. The Pharisee, on the other hand, was not equipped to show compassion. He had not yet received the love of God into his own heart by recognizing his need for forgiveness; therefore, he had nothing of Christ's love to offer the woman. It's for this reason Jesus said to Simon, "Therefore, I tell you, her many sins have been forgiven—as her great love has shown. But whoever has been forgiven little loves little" (Luke 7:47).

Heartless: Addicted

The final stage of becoming a Pharisee is when self-righteous attitudes develop into a type of judgmentalism that is outright heartless. At this point, the person is no longer merely intoxicated with spiritual pride, or failing to balance moral judgments with compassion, but has reached such an extreme level of darkness that rivals the worst kind of addiction—so controlled by a particular substance or lifestyle that they are willing to act out in ways that are well beyond what is considered normal human behavior.

Paul did not paint a rosy picture regarding what he was like prior to salvation. He referred to himself as a "blasphemer and a persecutor and a violent man" who showed "no mercy" for those who opposed his worldview. His religious addiction had turned him into a Pharisaical monster who sought to destroy Christianity without any concern for human life. Paul was responsible for stoning the first Christian martyr and worked to put ordinary believers, both men and women, in prison. He was the first-century equivalent of a notorious modern-day terrorist.

Paul said that his behavior was the result of being "extremely zealous for the traditions" of his fathers" (Galatians 1:14). In other words, he was guided by a strong conviction that his views about God were correct; therefore, anything or anyone who opposed his view was an enemy of God. Paul failed to see the truth that those in opposition to his beliefs were still the objects of God's love. When upholding traditions and defending our beliefs supersedes the dignity of humanity, we are being controlled by an ideology that is contrary to the character of God. It's a dangerous thing when the ends justify the means, especially in the name of God.

I was a sophomore in college when I decided to elevate my status as a professional sinner. I had spent several years prior to that season living quietly before the Lord, but like many young people in college, I took the ill-advised step of testing God's boundaries. A group of buddies was getting ready to party, and I was determined to join them in the fun. As we were about to leave, I heard the Holy Spirit impress strongly in my spirit, *Don't go! Don't go!* It was such a strong impression that I felt compelled to verbally respond to the Lord, "No, I'm going!"

After several days of partying and trying to ignore my guilt, I woke up at about two o'clock in the morning feeling completely alone in the universe. I walked into the bathroom and looked at my reflection in the mirror . . . and didn't like what I saw. Testing God in this way was unchartered territory for me. I was acting like a spoiled teenage boy willing to take his parents' car and leave for the weekend against their expressed warning. Except I had committed cosmic treason by going against the warning of the Holy Spirit. No good parent would allow his or her teenager to get away with such behavior without some type of severe punishment. I was scared that my punishment would involve being kicked out of heaven forever.

I walked out of the bathroom and made my way to the living room. During this time in my life, I wasn't grounded in Scripture, but I did know how to pray. I got down on my knees and cried out to the Lord. Even though I felt a thousand miles away from God, I called out to Him anyway. I will never forget what happened next. At the very moment I opened my mouth to pray, the Lord showered me with love, acceptance, and affirmation. I felt a powerful rush of Holy Spirit energy flow through me—all the way up my body and back down. God has responded to me this way only a few times in my life. However, at this moment, I needed to know that I was not forever banished from His presence. The powerful response from God that morning let me know that I was loved, forgiven, and safely in His arms.

Now let's travel back in time to the first century and examine what happened to the woman caught in adultery. Early one morning, Jesus was teaching in the temple courts in front of a crowd of people. While He was in the middle of speaking, some Pharisees dragged before the crowd a woman who was caught sleeping with a man. They said to Jesus, "Teacher, this woman was caught in the act of adultery. In the Law Moses commanded us to stone such women. Now what do you say?" (John 8:4–5).

There is no getting around the Pharisees' sinister motives. They had no intention of upholding the moral law but instead worked their scheme in a way that brought the most amount of public shame, humiliation, and embarrassment to the woman. They could have handled the situation in a private setting, but that would not have satisfied their vindictive agenda. Also, many scholars believe that the Pharisees must have arranged in advance for some spies to catch the woman in the act of adultery. Was the man she was sleeping with one of the Pharisees? Simply put, in the eyes of the religious leaders, the woman was nothing more than a pawn in their diabolical scheme to take down Jesus.

We have seen over the centuries how this type of addiction makes people feel justified for doing heartless things to other people. I know believers who, even after repenting behind closed doors for a private failure, have been publicly shamed in front of their churches. I have seen videos of preachers openly scold people during a church service. I have seen arrogant young pastors chastise other believers on public social media threads. We've all heard stories about visitors being rebuked for not wearing appropriate clothes in church. As the Barna Group study reveals, many self-described Christians have no reservations when it comes to rebuking, dismissing, alienating, and acting heartless toward people who stand in the way of their religious dogmas.

We need our leaders, people, and churches to repent from these behaviors and turn to Jesus for healing from the addiction. The love I experienced in my college apartment that morning is the same love that Jesus showed the woman caught in adultery. It's true that she broke the law and deserved capital punishment in the same way that my sins also deserved punishment, but Jesus did not come into the world to condemn people. He came to save people who already stand condemned.

For the sake of attracting people to Jesus, may we realign our hearts with the heart of Jesus. May we work to build people up, not tear them down. May we offer grace to those who struggle with a particular vice or sin. May we finally shed ourselves from the same religious/Pharisaical spirit that fought against the ministry and authority of Jesus. We must remove our lights from under the cover of self-righteousness, judgmentalism, and heartlessness to attract more people to Jesus.

Chapter 4

Brand Values

If people believe they share values with a brand, they will stay loyal to the brand.

HOWARD SCHULTZ[9]

Now that we have identified the brand image challenge that adversely affects the public perception of the Christian faith, we must shift our focus to the solution. This requires a closer look at another term used by marketers: *brand values*. Brand values represent the internal attitudes, principles, and behaviors that influence everything a brand does to accomplish its mission. We must not mistake brand values as merely sentimental ideas that make us feel more virtuous. On the contrary, brand values are essential to every mission-critical factor that impacts our ability to attract people to Jesus.

For example, Facebook seeks to create value by giving people the *power to build community and bring the world closer together*. To accomplish its mission, the company has established an internal culture that is driven by five core brand values:[10]

1. Be Bold

2. Focus on Impact

3. Move Fast

4. Be Open

5. Build Social Value

These brand values define the internal character of the organization that is needed to achieve its objectives. To underscore the importance of brand values, consider how Facebook's internal culture might impact their control over the sensitive data of billions of users, or how they affect national elections. "Be Bold" comes with the idea of taking risks in a competitive landscape, but at what point does a company's actions become irresponsible with user data? "Focus on Impact" seeks to address the most important priorities of the company, but is child safety a top priority? "Move Fast" might work to assist the company in launching new policies, but have they taken the time to weigh the implications of their policies against its impact on free speech?

Apple gained world dominance by driving the brand value of innovation that helped the company achieve historic user-experience advancements. As a result, the company has earned enormous trust with their customer base, many who are passionate and even religious brand ambassadors. Steve Jobs, the founder of Apple, once said, "Marketing is about values. This is a very complicated world; it's a very noisy world. And we're not going to get a chance to get people to remember much about us. And so we have to be clear about what we want them to know about us."[11] I would argue that if brand values are important in the business world to create memorable impressions with the general public, they are even more important in the context of attracting people to Jesus.

In 2010, Patrick Doyle was hired as the chief executive officer for Domino's Pizza during a time when the company's stock price was slipping. The growing sentiment among the general public was that Domino's Pizza was no longer making good pizza. You don't need a PhD in marketing to conclude that bad-tasting food is not the recipe for success when you're a pizza establishment. You may remember the commercials that confronted the problem head on. Normally, advertisements focus on the benefits of purchasing a product, but this campaign focused on what had gone terribly wrong. One commercial showed unfiltered comments made by several focus group members: "Worst pizza I ever had"; "The sauce tastes like ketchup"; "The crust tastes like cardboard."[12] The advertising campaign was designed to acknowledge the problem—bad-tasting pizza—and promise better results going forward.

Branding always works from the inside out, so if there's a brand values problem on the inside, it will always result in a brand image problem on the outside. In this case, Domino's Pizza was not living up to its internal values: *Produce the best for less* and *We are not ordinary, we are exceptional.*[13] As a result, the general public lost confidence in the company's ability to deliver on its most basic promise. Whereas Old Spice had a brand image problem on the outside, Domino's Pizza was dealing with a brand values problem on the inside. Somewhere along the way, the company lost focus on what made them great.

Patrick Doyle had the vision to successfully lead the company back to dominance. He understood that a renewed sense of clarity and focus on the company's internal brand values would help them reclaim lost market share. As a result, Domino's Pizza was revitalized from within the company. They rolled up their sleeves to create a much better tasting pizza and developed the most robust digital ordering platform in the industry. It was through a renewed focus on their internal brand values that propelled Domino's Pizza back into position as the second-largest pizza company in the United States.

In the context of the Christian faith, the brand image problem we're seeking to improve is the direct result of losing focus on the internal brand values of the gospel. We have an incredible opportunity to attract people to Jesus as we keep an eye toward His return. As the world grows increasingly dangerous, desperate, and divided, we can shine even brighter. I implore every believer to reconsider the brand values of the gospel and learn how they are designed to operate powerfully through the lives of everyday people.

Love, Joy, and Peace

If we apply the same methodologies used in business to define the brand values of the gospel, we recognize that *love, joy*, and *peace* represent the divine characteristics that are meant to shape the attitudes and behaviors of every authentic Christian. These brand values are designed to influence the way believers think, live, and impact others. Galatians 5:22–23 offer the complete list—"The fruit of the Spirit is *love, joy, peace*, patience, kindness, goodness, faithfulness, gentleness, and self-control"—but many scholars agree that the first three values mentioned in the list embody all of the values.

Before we go any further on this subject, it's crucial to understand that we cannot produce the brand values of the gospel through human strength. Instead, it helps to think of the values as God's divine character flowing through regular people. This applies to every authentic believer, at every stage of life, no matter the circumstances. Even during the most challenging times, we are promised access to the divine brand values that come directly from God. No matter what's happening, whether good or bad, the fruit of the Spirit represents the evidence that God is operating powerfully through our lives.

This point was underscored when Jesus and the disciples were caught in a severe storm as they traveled across the Sea of Galilee on their way to visit the demoniac. It's fascinating to note that Jesus was asleep in the stern of the boat while the other men were panicking for their lives. You can feel the perplexity of the disciples when they woke Jesus. "Teacher, don't you care if we drown?" (Mark 4:38). Sometimes it might appear that God does not care when difficult things are happening around us. It's in these moments when the brand values of the gospel often go missing. However, Jesus demonstrated that we have access to supernatural love, joy, and peace no matter the circumstances.

The verse says, "He got up, rebuked the wind and said to the waves, 'Quiet! Be Still!' Then the wind died down and it was completely calm" (Mark 4:39). This was quite an impressive miracle, indeed. We see that even the natural elements were subject to the commands of Jesus. However, I am convinced that Jesus demonstrated something even more significant by sleeping in the stern of the boat during the storm. Perhaps the entire point was to show the disciples that they, too, had access to that same peace? After all, if Jesus can bring supernatural peace to a raging storm on the sea, He can certainly bring supernatural peace to a distressed human heart. God wants our hearts to remain quiet and still no matter the circumstances, but we simply can't make that happen on our own. It's for this reason Jesus said, "Peace I leave with you; my peace I give you" (John 14:27).

Do you remember when you first got saved, or when God met you in the most personal way during a time when you needed Him the most? These moments have a way of generating explosive spiritual fruit in our lives. We are often overcome with a deep recognition of God's personal love for us. We might lay our heads down on the pillow and enjoy the sweetest sleep or overflow with an unshakable sense of joy, knowing that we are forgiven. We might also have more love and patience to offer other people. The impact of experiencing God in this way can last hours, days, weeks, or even months in our lives.

I am convinced the reason we overflow with the brand values of the gospel during these moments is not because we are flexing our spiritual prowess muscles but because our minds are temporarily renewed to the reality of what salvation means. We have become recipients of the goodness of God experientially, and, therefore, our awareness of His character and presence is better known and understood. Love, joy, and peace are not something we can achieve on our own. We can't rely on rules, ceremonies, or rituals to attain these qualities. Simply put, it's impossible to legislate or manufacture the fruit of the Spirit. These divine qualities can be accessed only by trusting in the spiritual source that is greater and more powerful than ourselves.

In the same way, we are also susceptible to being influenced by carnal thoughts that produce attitudes and behaviors that do not reflect the brand values of the gospel. We can easily get caught up in distractions, circumstances, and temptations. We often lose sight of how God feels about us and fail to live out the divine purpose for our lives. Inevitably, when this happens, the brand values of the gospel are replaced with far less attractive qualities, such as outbursts of wrath, sexual sins, and other carnal behaviors. It's in these moments we are allowing our lights to remain hidden under the cover of carnal thinking.

Moments before leaving on a business trip, I spoke with my wife about a spiritual relapse I was experiencing. Something was robbing me of the "joy unspeakable and full of glory" that is promised in the Bible. I was supposed to experience joy. I wanted to experience joy. However, the brand value of joy was conspicuously missing from my life. I was desperate to reclaim my spiritual freedom—so we prayed together. After a few minutes of prayer, a hopeful message was delivered through my wife. "I see you praising God and overflowing with joy in the near future," she said with confidence. I knew enough about my wife to know that God was speaking through her at that moment. During my drive from Seattle, Washington, to Portland, Oregon, I considered how God might restore my joy. I'm embarrassed to admit what I was thinking at the time, but for a fleeting moment, I considered that finances might be involved. "Maybe I'm about to get promoted, or blessed with a new car?" That notion could not have been further from the truth.

Over the next few days, I stumbled upon a Bible teacher who was masterful at articulating the blessings of the new covenant. God used this man to spark a renewed passion in me that caused me to go deeper in my study of the gospel. For the next several months, I spent hours each day learning, reading, and researching. I was relentless in my pursuit to answer questions that lingered stubbornly in the back of my mind. I am an obsessive thinker by nature, which can get me into trouble when my thoughts are pointed in the wrong direction. Thankfully, God was in the process of turning my obsessive thoughts in the right direction.

As my mind was being renewed to the finished work of Christ, something unexpected happened: I experienced a powerful resurgence of joy. Through the process of studying the new covenant, I was replacing harmful religious thoughts with new thoughts that were rooted in what Christ had done for me. When we allow the truth to penetrate deep into our hearts, it's impossible for fear, uncertainty, and depression to remain. By replacing my carnal thoughts with the truths in the gospel, I was no longer fixated on trying to earn God's approval or make up for my past sins. Instead, I was learning how to stand firmly on the promises of God, which resulted in a renewal of love, joy, and peace.

Paul described the process I went through: "Those who live according to the flesh have their minds set on what the flesh desires; but those who live in accordance with the Spirit have their minds set on what the Spirit desires" (Romans 8:5). In other words, the fruit of the Spirit is the result of a mind-set that develops when our thoughts are renewed to the truth. We must not underestimate the important role our minds play regarding walking in the fruit of the Spirit. A carnal mind-set will always produce carnal results, whereas a spiritual mind-set will always produce spiritual results. We often associate carnality with sexual sins or other egregious acts, which is entirely accurate; but we must not fail to recognize that allowing ourselves to be controlled by feelings of condemnation and self-loathing are also the result of carnal thinking.

Beauty for Ashes

Many people have been deeply scarred and feel that nothing has the power to take them out of the ashes and into spiritual victory. You may be thinking that all this love, joy, and peace stuff sounds nice, but you are simply too wounded for this to work in your life. I used to think the same way, but today I am living proof that all things are possible with God. I want to share with you from personal experience that no matter how wounded, broken, or afraid you might feel right now, Jesus has the power to restore your soul. I can testify that God specializes in turning brokenness into something beautiful—because it happened with me.

My story began on a tragic day that produced wounds in my soul that seemed insurmountable at times. My mother and her three children moved to the United States before I was conceived. When the day of my birth arrived, no relatives or friends were in the country to help, so my three siblings were taken to the playground across the street from the hospital. My siblings were excited to meet their baby brother that day and waited patiently for me to be born. Little did they know that everything was about to change in their lives.

The doctors and social workers quickly recognized that my mother was not mentally stable or in a suitable condition to care for her newborn child, let alone her three older children, who were waiting at the playground. As a result, my siblings did not meet their baby brother that day. I was placed into foster care, and my mother lived in a treatment center for the remainder of her life. Although my siblings tried to stay together, they lived much of their lives in separate foster homes and had difficult childhoods, to say the least. Thirty-two years later, I met my biological siblings for the first time. They told me that our mother had passed away many years before.

The difficulties we experience in life have a way of shaping how we perceive ourselves and the world around us. Although I was eventually adopted by an incredible family, growing up in a world with no biological associations created significant damage deep within my soul. I was always an optimistic person with an appreciation for life, but on the inside, something was broken. The process of being separated from my family and not knowing any blood relatives created a void in my heart that required help from above to heal. I lacked a sense of acceptance and identity, even though my adoptive family did everything they could to love and accept me.

We can easily avoid our struggles when we're young, but they eventually catch up to us. We often have fractures deep within our souls that require additional help from the Holy Spirit to bring healing. In addition to battling fierce bouts of anxiety related to PTSD, I also contended with rejection issues that often accompany people who have been adopted. I found it difficult to believe that I was truly accepted by my heavenly Father. I didn't realize what was happening to me at the time, but my problems were tied directly to subconscious thinking patterns that caused me to feel rejected. Becoming a Christian does not automatically remove problems from our lives.

One night in my bedroom when I was about eight, I started thanking God for no apparent reason. Nobody in my life modeled this behavior for me, and I didn't know to pray using the name of Jesus. However, something was turning in my heart that recognized God was in the middle of my family situation. I thanked Him for placing me in a safe home. I thanked Him for sending me to a loving family. After several minutes of thanking God, my heart began to grow increasingly more sincere. It was then I felt the powerful presence of the Holy Spirit envelop me. The presence was so tangible and unexpected that it caused me to stop speaking. I knew without a shadow of a doubt that God had visited me in my bedroom that night. It was truly my burning bush moment.

Over time, I was able to connect the dots and realize that during my prayer, I was born again and received the gift of the Holy Spirit. However, even though I had such a powerful conversion, I still struggled to experience the spiritual liberty promised in the gospel. The fractures in my soul fought against the love and affirmation that God poured into my life. I often questioned my salvation and wondered how God really felt about me. At one point, I was so overcome with feelings of condemnation that I convinced myself there was no more hope. I believed that I was going to hell and there was no way back. I spent months battling through depression and intense spiritual warfare, believing that I had been rejected by my heavenly Father.

Many believers struggle with thoughts that lead to feelings of condemnation and rejection. If you find yourself in a similar place of spiritual defeat, constantly wondering how God feels about you or trying to earn His approval, please know that Jesus is greater than your current struggles. You will experience love, joy, and peace as you go through the process of untangling yourself from carnal thinking patterns and replacing them with a clear understanding of the finished work of Christ. It happened for me; it will happen for you.

The Problem of Legalism

When I was struggling to believe that I was accepted by my heavenly Father, it wasn't because something was wrong with God; rather, it was because something was wrong with my thinking. I had already accepted Jesus as my personal Savior, which meant that love, joy, and peace belonged to me. The problem was that my soul needed to catch up with the reality of what God had already done in my life. I had fallen into a way of thinking that based my value, identity, and salvation on how well I could spiritually perform. In short, I was influenced by subtle but deadly thoughts that have their origin in legalism. These thoughts are still very prevalent in the lives of many believers.

Legalism is a way of relating to God that is based on conformity to laws, rules, and religious moral codes. Even the most subtle forms of legalism originate from the premise that our performance determines our status with God. It's important to note that although legalism drives some people to think like a Pharisee, it has the opposite effect on other people. I was the perfect candidate to allow the same faulty thoughts to drive me into a perpetual state of fear, depression, and spiritual burnout. I worked extremely hard to please God and, in the process, spent many years of my life not enjoying Him. Whether legalism causes you to think like a Pharisee, or if you are working hard to earn God's approval, the problem of legalism renders every believer ineffective at reflecting the brand values of the gospel.

Believers invite legalism into their lives because they have not yet understood and internalized the blessings of the new covenant, which we will examine later in this book. For those with a sincere desire to follow the Bible, it's quite easy to fall into the legalism trap. After all, many large portions of Scripture reference laws, rules, and moral commands, and every authentic believer wants to honor God through behavior. However, we miss the point entirely when we put our trust in following the rules that are written in the Bible. Jesus said it this way: "You study the Scriptures diligently because you think that in them you have eternal life. These are the very Scriptures that testify about me, yet you refuse to come to me to have life" (John 5:39–40). In other words, the power that is needed to have eternal life and live victoriously on this side of the cross is not found in a series of rules; it's found in a Person.

As the founder and lead pastor of Imagine Church, I make it a priority to teach new visitors how we do life together as a community. I want them to know up front that we may not perfectly align with the same teachings they heard growing up. We have a clear spiritual growth vision for our members that is centered on the new covenant. As a result, many people are not accustomed to the ministry nuances we embrace. The feedback we receive from new visitors is almost always positive; however, we will occasionally hear from people who have a more difficult time replacing their old thinking patterns. It can be challenging for those who have been entrenched in legalistic environments to think a different way.

New Wineskins

Jesus showed us why it can be difficult for people to break away from legalistic thoughts with the healing of the blind man. This was the same man we talked about in chapter two, who was thrown out of the temple by the religious leaders. Jesus did the most unusual thing by spitting in the blind man's eyes when He performed the miracle. This would certainly get the attention of legalistic people today and would probably get Jesus kicked out of most churches. However, if we want to free ourselves from the bondage of legalism, we must learn to embrace spiritual things that appear foolish on the outside. The message of the gospel is foolishness to those who are perishing, but it's the power of God for those who are being saved.

Jesus asked the man if he could see anything after spitting in his eyes. This question was asked to set up a powerful illustration about spiritual vision. At this point, the man could see people walking around, but he described them as looking like trees. In other words, his eyes were partially opened but his vision was not yet fully restored. It was only after Jesus touched the man a second time that he was completely healed and could see everything clearly. It's important to note that it was not by accident that Jesus performed the miracle in stages. If we think that Jesus could muster up only enough power to get the man halfway healed after the first touch, we're missing the point of the illustration entirely.

The reason for the unusual nature of the miracle is based on what happened before the blind man was brought to Jesus. Jesus had been ministering to a large crowd of people for several days. When it was time to send the crowd away, He was concerned that many of the people would faint from exhaustion because they hadn't eaten for a while and didn't have any food. Despite the lack of resources that was available to the disciples, Jesus instructed them to distribute the food anyway. Miraculously, with only seven loaves of bread and some fish, the disciples fed more than four thousand people. The lesson of the miracle is abundantly clear. Jesus is more than able to provide natural resources to those who are in need.

Not long after the miracle, Jesus warned the disciples to watch out for the yeast of the Pharisees. He wanted to protect them against the root of spiritual pride that had caused the religious leaders to puff up with hypocrisy. However, the disciples missed the point and thought that Jesus was concerned about not having bread for their journey. After hearing their discussion, Jesus asked them: "Why are you talking about having no bread? Do you still not see or understand? Are your hearts hardened? Do you have eyes but fail to see, and ears but fail to hear?" (Mark 8:17–18). Keep in mind, this conversation happened only a short time after the disciples were responsible for miraculously distributing food to thousands of people.

After Jesus expressed His frustration to the disciples about not having eyes to see, they arrived at the destination where the blind man was located. The partial healing was used to demonstrate that in the same way the blind man did not see natural things clearly, the disciples did not see spiritual truths clearly. In other words, Jesus used the healing as an object lesson to underscore the importance of spiritual eyesight. Interestingly, it was the failure of the disciples to understand Jesus's teaching about the dangers of legalism that prompted the object lesson.

To the extent that we fail to see Jesus, everything else becomes blurry. To that end, I am convinced that many believers do not exemplify the brand values of love, joy, and peace because their eyesight is blurry from the subtle influences of legalism. It's possible to believe that Jesus is the Son of God but fail to understand the finished work of Christ. It's possible to hold the Bible in high regard but fail to grasp that we can't walk in the Spirit by keeping the rules. It's possible to be zealous for the things of

God but not operate according to knowledge. When it comes to unleashing the brand values of the gospel through our lives, we must be willing to see our way through the barriers of legalism that prevent our lights from shining.

I believe that God desires to release fresh insights into the hearts of people around the world. However, those who want to live free from the bondage of legalism must position themselves to receive the truths that are represented in the new covenant. We are no longer under the old system that relies on human strength; rather, we have received a new way to live that is based on the power of God. Jesus said it this way, "And no one pours new wine into old wineskins. Otherwise, the wine will burst the skins, and both the wine and the wineskins will be ruined. No, they pour new wine into new wineskins" (Mark 2:22). Many people in Jesus's time couldn't receive the fresh things that God was doing because the constraints of old thoughts, traditions, and religious structures kept them under the thumb of legalism. Likewise, Christians today are locked into performance-based living—legalism—rather than living in the freedom of Jesus's teaching.

If you are trapped within a performance mentality that keeps you from experiencing love, joy, and peace, be encouraged that many seasoned believers are learning for the first time what it means to live on this side of the cross. One gentleman told me that after attending a legalistic church for over twenty-five years, he was finally being set free. Another person told me that after thirty years of going to church, she is starting to understand the gospel for the first time. The same thing can happen for you. If you want to enjoy the brand values of the gospel and attract more people to Jesus, perhaps it's time to become a new wineskin. It's time to remove the bushel of legalism from your thinking and place your light on the lampstand of spiritual freedom.

Chapter 5

BRAND PROMISE

Your premium brand better be delivering something special,
or it's not going to get the business.

WARREN BUFFETT[14]

THE FIRST TIME I had the opportunity to ride in a BMW M series sportscar, I instantly realized that not all vehicles are created equal. I'm not an automobile enthusiast by any stretch of
the imagination, but everything about my experience riding in
that car confirmed that BMW certainly lived up to its promise of
delivering the Ultimate Driving Machine. In the world of marketing, a *brand promise* represents the commitment a company
makes to its customers. Any time we exchange money for a product or service, we should always expect to receive the full value
of what has been promised. It's a competitive landscape in every
industry, so the company that can deliver the most impressive
brand promise has the strongest advantage. It's for this reason
brands are always working to develop new and better solutions.

One of the most well-known brand promises in recent years
came from the auto insurance company called Geico. We've all
heard the now-famous promise: "15 minutes or less can save you
15 percent or more on car insurance." When the promise was
first released through a series of humorous advertisements, the

offer was notably superior to what other companies could deliver at the time. The idea of saving time and money while shopping for auto insurance was a novel proposition. The brand promise was made possible through the development of online technology that streamlined the process of purchasing insurance. As a result, the company made waves in the industry by surpassing All State Insurance as the second-largest auto insurance company in the United States. Geico achieved extraordinary results and succeeded at repositioning itself in the market—all because it lived up to a more compelling brand promise.

A similar thing happened when Netflix changed the way people rent movies. Instead of leaving the house to visit the local Blockbuster Video store, consumers could select videos on a website and have them shipped to their front doors. As online streaming technology improved, Netflix created a sophisticated on-demand experience. With just a few clicks of the mouse, people could watch movies instantly from the convenience of their homes. No more driving to the store or waiting for a product to arrive in the mail. The emergence of Netflix was the result of the company striving toward a more compelling brand promise.

It's worth noting that while Netflix was changing the way people rent movies, Blockbuster Video did not make any changes to its business model. There was a time when the brick-and-mortar solution was the best option to rent movies. However, the company's failure to recognize how the industry was changing eventually put them out of business. Blockbuster Video lost its dominant position in the marketplace and slowly faded away, becoming obsolete. In the world of business, the company that can provide the most credible, authentic, and compelling brand promise—and consistently keep the promise—has the best chance at success.

In the same way, there was a time when the rules-based way of relating to God was the most relevant option. Under the old covenant, the children of Israel were given the opportunity to live in covenant with God by adhering to a series of written commands. However, this system represented only a shadow of the good things to come and was not what God ultimately had in mind. Therefore, at the time of His sovereign choosing, Jesus became the mediator of a new and better covenant that resulted in a far superior brand promise. After hundreds of years of living under the strict demands of God's written law, the people were finally liberated from the drudgery of the rules-based system.

The events that transpired to bring about the new covenant represent the most significant events in human history and offer the greatest news the world has ever known. However, people get into trouble when they fail to make a clean transition from the old system to the new way of relating to God. Contrary to popular opinion, the new covenant does not represent a modified version of the old system. Neither is there any room to blend the systems. Instead, God established the new covenant to replace the rules-based approach with something radically different. Don't take it from me. Listen to the author of Hebrews emphasize how the advent of the new system made the first one obsolete: "By calling this covenant 'new,' he has made the first one obsolete, and what is obsolete and outdated will soon disappear" (Hebrews 8:13). To be clear, the first covenant was put out of business over two thousand years ago.

This change in covenants represents the most important factor when it comes to letting our lights shine on the lampstand of spiritual freedom. If we want to live free and attract people to Jesus, we must recognize how the divine marketing strategy hinges on our willingness to renew our minds to the blessings of the new covenant. Many believers do not realize the extent to which their spiritual lives are impacted by the subtle influences of the rules-based approach. Perhaps the most formidable obstacle that prevents believers from living the brand values of the gospel is getting caught somewhere between the old and new systems. Jesus died on the cross so that we might enjoy the incredible blessings of a new and better way of relating to God.

Old Covenant Brand Promise

Before we dive into the nuances of what makes the new covenant superior, we must first understand the basis for the old covenant's establishment in the first place. To explore this further, it helps to have a good idea of what that word *covenant* means in Scripture. In the original language, the word *covenant* was used in the same that we frequently use the word *contract* in modern society. It was an agreement made between two or more parties that included certain terms that must be met. For example, when you sign up for an account with Netflix, you are given access to a robust video library in exchange for a monthly subscription fee. If the required terms are satisfactorily met by both parties, everyone is happy.

Similarly, the contract between God and the children of Israel also came with required terms; however, the implications of the terms were far more consequential than a Netflix account. Essentially, the people were given a choice between living under a blessing or living under a curse. The option they chose was entirely dependent on their ability to follow a series of written commands. Moses provided a general summary of the old covenant requirements: "See, I am setting before you today a blessing and a curse—the blessing if you obey the commands of the Lord your God that I am giving you today; the curse if you disobey the commands of the Lord your God and turn from the way that I command you today by following other gods, which you have not known" (Deuteronomy 11:26–28).

As we explore the required terms in more detail, it's important to note the level of confidence the people had in their ability to uphold the contract: "We will do everything the Lord has said" (Exodus 19:8), they proclaimed. In response to the people's verbal commitment to the Lord, God summoned Moses to the top of Mount Sinai to receive the Ten Commandments. As it turned out, the Ten Commandments were not as easy to follow as one might assume. The people needed additional guidance to uphold the true purity, purpose, and spirit of the moral laws. Therefore, the Lord added more than six hundred additional civic and ceremonial laws to the list. As the people would soon find out, pleasing God through their human ability was always an impossible endeavor.

The confidence the people had in their ability to follow the contract offers profound insight into the purpose of the rules-based system. Something about the human condition makes it difficult for people to recognize that they can't live up to the perfect standard of God. In this case, Moses did not even make it down the mountain before the people had already violated the first and most important command: You shall have no other gods before me. They broke the command by worshipping a statue that Aaron fashioned using golden platters, goblets, their wives' earrings, and other articles they'd received from the Egyptians. They also did the unthinkable by giving credit to the statue for their miraculous deliverance out of slavery. "These are your gods, Israel, who brought you up out of Egypt" (Exodus 32:8). In virtually no time, the people failed to adhere to the covenant's required terms in the most egregious way.

What happened next can be described as a type of tragic symbolism that represents the brand promise of the law-based system. As a result of breaking the terms of the old covenant, about three thousand people *died* after Moses came down from the mountain. Notably, another type of symbolism that represents the brand promise of the new covenant happened when Peter preached at the inauguration of the new system (Pentecost). About three thousand people were *saved on that day*. The implications of these two contrasting events could not be more obvious—the brand promise of the old covenant is *death*, whereas the brand promise of the new covenant is *life*.

Rules-Based Living

Many people claim to have made a clean transition to the new covenant but continue to live as though they are still under the old system. By doing so, such people forfeit the power that is available to live a victorious life on this side of the cross. Consider for a moment how the concept of rules-based living is consistent with the way most people operate around the world. When you boil the methodology down to its foundation, every secular society and pagan religion march to a similar philosophical drumbeat: If we do what is good, we will be rewarded for being good. If we do what is bad, we will be rewarded for being bad. This principle, also known as cause and effect, is the golden rule of religion. We have been conditioned to think this way since birth; therefore, anything that challenges its basic premise can be more difficult to accept.

To address this issue, the apostle Paul introduced an interesting phrase in several of his writings that provides context to why the new way of relating to God is necessary. He wanted to demonstrate that adhering to the rules-based system, although it appeared spiritual to the naked eye, was no better than following the same basic patterns of secular society. "What I am saying is that as long as an heir is underage, he is no different from a slave, although he owns the whole estate. The heir is subject to guardians and trustees until the time set by his father. So also, when we were underage, we were in slavery under the *elemental spiritual forces of the world*" (Galatians 4:3).

Paul wrote this letter to establish the importance of grace compared with the law during a time when dangerous law-based teachers were infiltrating the church. The false teachers were trying to convince the people that following certain rules was required in addition to trusting Christ. Paul used the phrase *elemental spiritual forces of the world* to warn the people that reverting to the law-based system would result in an elementary lifestyle that held no superiority over the basic patterns of the world. Paul insisted that he received the gospel of grace through divine revelation that came directly from God. Certainly, he must have received something far more profound, magnificent, and powerful than the rudimentary approach that any pagan society could offer.

Before we go any further, let me make this next point loud and clear. I am not saying that the law is unholy, does not exist, or does not serve a purpose. On the contrary, the law represents the perfect and holy standard of the living God. Furthermore, the brand value of the law—namely, death—is critical to the process of salvation. The need to expose the moral depravity of humanity and make everyone guilty before God is necessary to understand that we can't rely on human ability to make it to heaven. It's for this reason Paul referred to the law as the "ministry of death" and the "ministry of condemnation." The law is effective at producing death and condemnation with great perfection. However, it provides no support, no remedy, and no escape from the spiritual death that it causes and the sentence of condemnation that it renders.

As Paul states far more eloquently, the law functions as our guardian, or tutor, that holds us captive as slaves until we recognize our need for a Savior. Its primary purpose is to minister death and condemnation so that we might come to the end of ourselves and trust Jesus for salvation. In addition, Paul is emphasizing that across the corridor of redemptive history, the old covenant served the purpose of guiding the people of God through their adolescent years, or when they were "underage." However, those who are in Christ have graduated from adolescence and reached full maturity. Therefore, the law is holy, alive, and necessary up to the point of salvation. After we are saved, however, we have received a new way to live that does not involve the law.

Despite this important spiritual truth, many precious believers keep turning to the law for empowerment in their daily living. Such an approach is like pouring gasoline on a fire to try to put it out. Paul informs us that the law does not produce righteous living but, in fact, has the reverse effect. "But sin, seizing the opportunity afforded by the commandment, produced in me every kind of coveting. For apart from the law, sin was dead" (Romans 7:8). In other words, if you tell a child that it's wrong to touch the cookie jar, the cookies are more likely to be gone by morning. And in the process, the child is now guilty of breaking a law that did not exist prior to the command. To be clear, the purpose of the law is to expose our moral inabilities, not to help us live victoriously. Many people have a difficult time receiving the counterintuitive nature of this truth, so they cling to the law as a safety net for daily living.

I remember watching Mike Tyson fight when he was in his prime. For several years, nobody could make it out of the first round against the guy. He was too fast, powerful, and explosive for even the strongest opponent to withstand. Try to imagine getting into the ring against Mike Tyson during his prime. I don't know about you, but that sounds like a terrifying proposition to me. I would get knocked out within the first ten seconds. It's the same idea being under the rules-based system of the law. Not even the most disciplined person can meet the stringent challenge. If you get into the ring against the law, you will get knocked out in the first round every time—as did the children of Israel.

We must recognize that law-based living is not how we are designed to live on this side of the cross. The harder we try to manufacture what only God can do through us, the faster we invite spiritual bondage into our lives. When we attempt to *do more* and *be more* and *try harder* in our pursuit to please God, we set ourselves up for spiritual burnout. We should take courage in knowing that the law has already completed its powerful work in our lives and that we have now received a new way to live that is far more effective. Rest assured, we have been set free from the curse of the law (Galatians 3:13); we are not under the law, but under grace (Romans 6:14); and Christ is the end of the law for everyone who believes (Romans 10:4).

Jesus is the only person in human history who took on the law and came out victorious. In fact, the law was no match for the Son of God. Jesus did not commit any sinful acts and fulfilled every requirement of the law to perfection. As a result, He earned the heavyweight championship belt that is required to be in right standing with God under the law. And here's the most amazing part of the story: Instead of putting the belt inside a heavenly trophy case to show off to the angels, He placed it around your waist! Jesus took care of the law so that you don't have to step into the ring and get beat up anymore. His victory paved the way to replace the brand promise of death with a new way of relating to God that gives life.

Whenever I share these insights, I typically get one of two responses. Either people let out a huge sigh of relief, or they begin to wrestle with a few common objections. *Doesn't this give people a license to sin? How am I supposed to live without rules, laws, and moral codes?* Don't be alarmed. If you are struggling with these questions, it means you are getting closer to a more accurate understanding of the gospel. Keep in mind that similar objections were brought before Paul. We will resolve these issues later in the book. For now, let's rally around the one truth that has the power to set you free: The law brings death, but the Spirit gives life!

New Covenant Brand Promise

The children of Israel were given every opportunity to enjoy a blessed life while living under the law, but it did not work out favorably for either party. The people went through a constant cycle of failures, punishments, and recommitments that became the hallmark of the old covenant. They also experienced seasons of blessings, but the level of uncertainty that transpired was not the long-term plan God had in mind. Something was fundamentally flawed with the old system that cried out for a better solution.

The author of Hebrews offers the most straightforward explanation for why the old system was not sufficient: "For if there had been nothing wrong with the first covenant, no place would have been sought for another. But *God found fault with the people*" (Hebrews 8:7–8). The Lord had every right to command holy living and certainly wanted the people to experience a blessed life. However, the system failed because the people did not continue in the covenant. As a result, the author of Hebrews describes the old system as "weak and useless" insomuch as its success was dependent on the ability of the people. In short, the purpose of the old system was successful at exposing the weakness of humanity, but it did not go any further. Therefore, a new way forward was sought that could solve the fundamental flaw that exists within fallen humanity.

Steve Jobs is one of the greatest visionaries the world has ever seen. By the age of thirty, he had already revolutionized personal computing and risen to stardom as one of the wealthiest and most successful celebrities in the world. It's hard to believe that after so much success, he was forced out of Apple by its board of directors in 1985. After that, Apple had a few successful years but eventually experienced a sharp decline in growth. By the year 1993, the decline had reached a breaking point where the company was on life support. Margins were evaporating and the company's stock value was suffering dramatically. Finally, in 1996, Apple approached Steve Jobs and asked him to take over again as its leader.

After a few months at the helm, Steve Jobs spoke at the Worldwide Developers Conference in San Jose, California, where he talked about his vision for the company. Whenever a leader starts the process of creating systemic change, there will always be at least one skeptic in the crowd. During the question-and-answer portion of the event, a man in the audience expressed his frustration that the company's vision did not include the use of a technology called OpenDoc. Steve Jobs gave a brilliant response that in many ways defined his philosophy for creating innovative products:

> One of the hardest things when you're trying to effect change is that people like this gentleman are right in some areas. I'm sure that there are some things Open-Doc does, probably even more that I'm not familiar with, that nothing else out there does. The hardest thing is how does that fit into a cohesive, larger vision that's going to

allow you to sell ten billion dollars in product per year? One of the things I've always found is that you've got to *start with the customer experience and work backwards* to the technology.[15]

In the world of business, product development is the process that seeks to identify a customer need, conceptualize a solution, and then build a product. Unlike the critical guy in the audience, Jobs understood that identifying the customer need first and then working backward to the technology would result in the best product. His focus on the user experience is why Apple products have a certain genius in their simplicity. The iPad is so easy to use that even the most technically challenged among us can enjoy the product. However, to create a better user experience, a company must take the burden off the shoulders of the end user and develop a more innovative solution.

In the same way, God created a cohesive larger vision to bring the most people into a secure, intimate, and enjoyable relationship with Himself. Although the rules-based approach did accomplish the goal of producing death and condemnation, it did not create the desired solution for daily living because it relied on old technology—namely, the fallen condition of humanity. In addition, the sacrificial system was a tedious process that worked to always remind the people of their sins. Therefore, God went about the most remarkable innovation the world has ever seen by reverse engineering a foolproof spiritual solution that solved the problem of fallen humanity. In short, instead of relying on the people to perform well enough to make the old system work, God put the needs of humanity first by doing the necessary work to create a superior product. As a result, the new covenant brand promise offers the blessing of eternal life to everyone who believes—with a guarantee the promise cannot be revoked. Also, we have received three new dynamic blessings that changed the way believers are designed to live victoriously on this side of the cross (more on that in the next chapter).

Impossible with Man; Possible with God

One day a man asked Jesus, "Teacher, what good thing must I do to get eternal life?" (Matthew 19:16). Like many people in modern society, the man believed that being a good person was the pathway to right standing with God. Therefore, in response, Jesus told him that he must keep the commandments to have eternal life. This response is noteworthy because scholars would accurately maintain that salvation comes only through faith in Jesus. However, this interaction took place before the new contract was put into motion. Keep in mind, it was the death of Jesus on the cross, not His birth, that ratified the new covenant. Therefore, Jesus was speaking to a person who was still under the law-based system.

Interestingly, after being told that he must keep the commandments, the man responded, "Which ones?" Jesus then replied with an abbreviated list of the moral laws, which included: do not murder, do not commit adultery, do not steal, do not give false testimony, do not dishonor your father and mother, and love your neighbor as yourself. Technically, it would have been possible for the man to inherit eternal life by keeping the commandments, but only if he were able to keep each law perfectly throughout his entire life. Of course, unless you are the Son of God, only those who are spiritually blind would believe they are morally perfect. Therefore, it would have been good for the man to reflect on his failures before responding. Instead, he continued the conversation by insisting that his moral track record was perfect. "All these I have kept. What do I still lack?" (Matthew 19:20). In short, the man did not recognize his need for a Savior.

When helping people see their shortcomings, the ministry of the law always gets the job done. Clearly, the initial list of commands did not get through to the man; therefore, Jesus turned up the heat by elevating the true spirit of the law: "If you want to be perfect, go, sell your possessions and give to the poor, and you will have treasure in heaven. Then come, follow me" (Matthew 19:21). This response went directly to the root of the wealthy man's moral issue and placed him at the crossroads of an important decision. Would he trust that Jesus was the most reliable option to secure his future, or would he continue to trust in his wealth, possessions, and community position? The man walked away from the conversation sorrowful because his soul was captivated by the strongholds of earthly riches. Once again, the ministry of death prevailed at exposing the moral depravity of humankind.

Jesus then turned to the disciples and explained that it's exceedingly difficult for a wealthy person to enter the kingdom of God. It was believed at the time that great wealth was a symbol of God's special favor on a person. Therefore, the disciples were astonished at the weight of the moment. If entering heaven was difficult for a wealthy person, who was believed to have special favor with God, what did that mean for everyone else? It's why the disciples asked, "Who then can be saved?" The impossibility of keeping the law had reached a crescendo right before the disciples' eyes. Jesus responded to their concern with a prophetic statement that captured the true essence of the new covenant and pointed to its soon coming: "What is impossible with man is possible with God" (Luke 18:27).

When the terms of the new contract were drafted in heaven, something had to change that would fulfill the requirements that had proven impossible with man. Brilliantly, God did the unthinkable by making a new contract that removed the people from the equation entirely. In other words, the stringent requirements of the contract were no longer binding between God and the people. Instead, the requirements of the new contract were binding between God and Himself. Paul describes the legal nature of the contract: "He forgave us all our sins, having canceled the charge of our *legal indebtedness*, which stood against us and condemned us; He has taken it away, nailing it to the cross" (Colossians 2:13–14). As a result, believers are the beneficiaries of a new and better contract that cannot fail because it's based on the performance and trustworthiness of God alone. What we were not able to accomplish, Jesus accomplished on our behalf so that we might receive the brand promise of eternal life.

Many people struggle to believe that what God accomplished is powerful enough to take them all the way to heaven. We often insert ourselves into the contract and worry that our performance will disqualify us from receiving the brand promise of eternal life. In these moments, we fail to recognize that believers are merely the beneficiaries of the contract. For example, if you are listed as the beneficiary of a life insurance policy, you will receive the financial advantage after the policyholder dies. The level of confidence you have in the financial benefit should be based on the financial strength of the company—not on the financial strength of the beneficiary. Similarly, every believer has received the spiritual advantage of eternal life. The confidence we should have in the fulfillment of the promise is founded on the moral strength of the Lord. To underscore this point, the author of Hebrews demonstrates that the new contract is backed with a guarantee that offers the greatest amount of hope to the beneficiary:

> Because God wanted to make the unchanging nature of his purpose very clear to the heirs of what was promised, he confirmed it with an oath. God did this so that, by two unchangeable things in which it is impossible for God to lie, we who have fled to take hold of the hope set before us may be greatly encouraged. (Hebrews 6:17–18)

The promise of eternal life would not be eternal if it ended prematurely. Therefore, the author of Hebrews demonstrates that almighty God represents both the Promisor and Guarantor of the promise. He alone makes eternal life possible and ensures the full delivery of the promise to every beneficiary. In short, since there can be no greater entity in the universe to ensure the veracity of a brand promise, believers can have great confidence in their eternal security. Jesus said it this way: "I give them eternal life, and they shall never perish; no one will snatch them out of my hand.

My Father, who has given them to me, is greater than all; no one can snatch them out of my Father's hand." (John 10:28–29).

The new covenant offers the most credible, authentic, and compelling brand promise anywhere in the universe and beyond. As you renew your mind to this incredible truth, you will rest in the finished work of Christ and attract more people to Jesus.

Chapter 6

Brand Integrity

Brand is just a perception, and perception will match reality over time.

ELON MUSK[16]

My opinion that BMW has lived up to the brand promise of creating the Ultimate Driving Machine would probably change if the company's website was poorly done, or if the repair centers were not capable of servicing the vehicles. Every business needs a compelling brand promise to succeed, but what good is a brand promise if the customer experience is not consistent? On this front, marketers use the term *brand integrity* to measure how well a company stays true to its promises across every customer touchpoint. As the innovative Elon Musk once said, "Perception will match reality over time." It's for this reason business executives carry a heavy responsibility to develop internal processes that maintain the integrity of the brand promise across the entire company.

I was surprised to learn that Nestlé is the largest food and beverage company in the world. I always thought they made good chocolate but had no idea they also have over two thousand separately branded products. Their products are sold in over 185 countries and include many items you might have in your kitchen right now: pizza, coffee flavoring, baby foods, meats, sparkling water, microwavable dinners . . . the list goes on. Considering the high volume of food and beverage products the company is responsible for producing and selling, as well as the number of people who consume their products around the world, Nestlé carries a certain responsibly related to the health and nutrition of its customers.

We live in a world in which many people are health conscience and aware of what they're putting in their bodies. Nestlé is smart to align itself with the nutritional values that are important to people. The company's mission statement promises to "enhance the quality of life and contribute to a healthier future."[17] Even their tagline supports the value of creating healthier lives: "Good food, Good life." It's safe to say that Nestlé has made a promise to uphold certain nutritional standards across their product line. However, if they want to create brand integrity with their consumers, they must follow through with internal processes that uphold their sacred pledge. The extent to which a company stays true to its brand promise is what ultimately determines brand integrity.

When eating candy bars and other junk food, most people are not looking for the healthiest options at the local minimart. However, in the year 2015, Nestlé made the controversial decision to remove artificial flavors and colors from more than 250 of its products. The changes were also applied to several of their famous candies, such as Butterfinger, Baby Ruth, and Crunch. Candy company executives know that some consumers believe healthy ingredients don't taste good. Therefore, Nestlé risked that a portion of their customer base might not be happy with the changes. However, they chose to stay true to their brand promise despite the potential backlash from certain consumers.

In the same way, if believers want to live free and attract people to Jesus, we must be willing to uphold the core principles of the new covenant across every aspect of our faith; otherwise, we will forfeit the brand integrity of the gospel. Paul wrote to the

Galatian church: "It is for freedom that Christ has set us free. Stand firm, then, and do not let yourselves be burdened again by a yoke of slavery" (Galatians 5:1). Paul was dealing with an influx of law-based teachers who were propagating concepts that did not represent the new covenant. The teachers insisted that salvation for the gentile believers required faith in Jesus plus circumcision. Salvation happens only when a person trusts in the finished work of Christ, therefore this teaching went against the message of the cross. We must never create a false gospel that is dependent on human effort.

It's worth noting that Paul was not dealing with a few laypersons in the church who didn't know any better. Some of the most influential spiritual leaders in the first century were caught in the deception. Paul writes that during a church banquet, James, the younger brother of Jesus, brought some of the law-based teachers to the meeting. When they arrived, every single Jewish person in attendance, including Peter, James, and Barnabas, segregated themselves from the gentile believers. They were sending a strong message that the gentile believers were not complete in their salvation because they did not adhere to the works of the law. The leaders were denying the importance of grace and compromising the brand integrity of the gospel.

The situation quickly spiraled out of control and became a pivotal moment in the history of the church. Not willing to allow the problem to continue, Paul took a bold stand in front of the entire group: "When I saw that they were not *acting in line with the truth of the gospel*, I said to Cephas in front of them all, 'You are a Jew, yet you live like a Gentile and not like a Jew. How is it, then, that you force Gentiles to follow Jewish customs?'" (2:14). This was not an issue of merely changing the seating arrangements in the banquet room to accommodate the sensibilities of the Jewish leaders. Instead, Paul stated they were not *acting in line with the truth of the gospel*. In other words, the Jewish leaders were responsible for corrupting the new covenant and putting the people they influenced back into bondage.

There will always be people who don't want to uphold the brand integrity of the gospel. Doing the works of the law has a certain appeal that makes us feel more in control of our lives. However, real spiritual problems arise when the principles of the new covenant are not taken seriously. People will begin to trust in their own ability to stay right with God because they fall into the fallacy that grace is not sufficient to live the Christian life. As a result, people seek to balance grace with the works of the law to decrease the power of sin, which, unfortunately, has the opposite effect in their lives. The key to living in triumph over fear, hardships, coping mechanisms, and temptations is found in Jesus alone.

New Covenant Blessings

When we were planning the launch of Imagine Church, I spent considerable time thinking about how to create a spiritual growth process that would not compromise the brand integrity of the gospel. I was fully aware of the law-based nuances that often sneak their way into the branding, messaging, and processes of the local church. Therefore, I wanted to create a system that was established on the new covenant and guarded against the tendency to rely on human strength. Before I explain how the spiritual growth process works, we must first review the blessings of the new covenant that provide the theological basis for the approach.

The new covenant is established upon three primary blessings that change how we think, live, and impact others on this side of the cross:

- New Creation
- Intimate Relationship
- Total Forgiveness

Each of these pillars offers a new spiritual reality that did not exist under the rules-based system. Despite this important truth, many believers continue to feel uneasy about making a full transition to the new covenant. You may sense in your heart that Christ has set you free but continue to live tired, defeated, and frustrated. However, as you internalize the blessings of the new covenant, you will find your true spiritual rest in Jesus Christ.

Blessing One: New Creation

The author of Hebrews is masterful at explaining the blessings of the new covenant. Specifically, the author shines a light on a prophecy that was spoken by the prophet Jeremiah during a time when the children of Israel were struggling under the rules-based system. The prophecy was designed to offer hope that a new and better covenant was on the horizon. "'The days are coming,' declares the Lord, 'when I will make a new covenant with the people of Israel and with the people of Judah. It will not be like the covenant I made with their ancestors when I *took them by the hand* to lead them out of Egypt, because they broke my covenant, though I was a husband to them,' declares the Lord" (Jeremiah 31:31–32).

Right out of the gate, the prophecy makes clear that life under the new system would be different. Specifically, God would no longer take people *by the hand* to lead them out of Egypt. At first glance, this phrase struck me as unusual because I enjoy leading my children across the street by the hand. However, this phrase was meant to illustrate how the old contract was based upon adherence to an external ethical system. To keep the people from going back into slavery, they were given the opportunity to live an *outside-in life* by keeping the rules.

However, in the same way that a toddler constantly veers away from its guardian when walking down the street, the people did not have the spiritual capacity to continue in the covenant. They required constant handholding because they could not overcome their spiritual condition. Therefore, the new solution would require something far more profound than keeping a series of external rules, ethics, and moral codes. As the prophecy continues, we are introduced to the first blessing of the new covenant known as *new creation*. As a result of this blessing, the internal problem that exists within the human condition has been resolved. "'This is the covenant I will make with the people of Israel after that time,' declares the Lord. '*I will put my law in their minds and write it on their hearts*'" (Jeremiah 31:33).

I told you earlier about the night in my bedroom when I felt the presence of the Holy Spirit. I was only a child at the time and had no theological basis to understand what the experience meant. I simply went to sleep and carried on with my life as if nothing changed, not realizing until many years later that I had become a new creation. That's not to say that accepting Jesus will always result in a powerful experience with the Holy Spirit. The point is that for several years I was a born-again Christian without knowing that I was a born-again Christian.

Looking back, however, my life was radically changed that night. A still small voice guided, comforted, and encouraged me from that moment forward. I seemed to have a deeper awareness of my sinful actions and a genuine desire to please God. I saw the world through a lens of faith and frequently spoke to the Lord in prayer. In short, I had an authentic faith and reliance upon God that was not the result of following rules. These things could happen in my life only because the Lord did a powerful work on the inside of me.

People tend to believe that Christianity is about doing and saying the right things, always making the right choices, or being a good person. However, the reality of salvation goes far beyond changing how we live on the outside. The process of becoming a new creation is a supernatural event whereby the Holy Spirit makes a person come alive spiritually. Jesus used the term *born again*. Paul used the term *new creation*. The point is that believers have received a new spiritual identity that is fully compatible with the righteousness of God. Whereas the old system was based on living an outside-in life by keeping the rules, the new system is based on living an inside-out life that flows from the believer's new spiritual identity. Paul said it this way, "Therefore, if anyone is in Christ, the new creation has come: The old has gone, the new is here!" (2 Corinthians 5:17).

Blessing Two: Intimate Relationship

I once held a Bible study at my home that caught the attention of my next-door neighbor. The first time she attended, we happened to be studying an event that took place under the leadership of Moses. I'll never forget the question my neighbor asked during the study: "Why did the people have it so much better under the old covenant? It must have been great to see the miracles and hear directly from the prophets." As I thought about how to respond, the Holy Spirit reminded me of the second primary blessing of the new covenant given through the prophet Jeremiah, known as *intimate relationship*.

"'I will be their God, and they will be my people. No longer will they teach their neighbor, or say to one another, "Know the Lord," because *they will all know me*, from the least of them to the greatest,' declares the Lord" (Jeremiah 31:33–34).

It may seem obvious today, but the idea of *knowing the Lord* was not the normative experience under the old system. Certain hand-selected leaders were given access to an intimate relationship with God because they were to help guide the people. Most of the people, however, had only a general knowledge about God. Their understanding was based on how the Lord interacted with the nation of Israel through prophecies and miraculous signs. As a result, it was natural for the people to develop a strong dependence on the leaders. In addition, the relational emphasis was focused on the Lord's protection over the nation at large. It's for this reason the people viewed the Lord primarily as their fortress, shield, and protector.

The blessing of *intimate relationship* changes the way believers relate to God on this side of the cross. It's true that we still need leaders who are gifted at teaching, guiding, and protecting God's people, but every believer has received the ultimate leader in the Holy Spirit. Although it's comforting to have a powerful fortress, shield, and protector in the Lord, every believer now enjoys an intimate relationship with a loving Father. Paul said it this way, "The Spirit you received does not make you slaves, so that you live in fear again; rather, the Spirit you received brought about your adoption to sonship. And by him we cry, 'Abba, Father'" (Romans 8:15).

Blessing Three: Total Forgiveness

Did your mother ever say those dreaded words to you growing up when you did something wrong? "Wait until your father gets home from work!" My dad was always a reasonable person, but if we pushed things too far, there was a good chance punishment was in store for us when he got home from work. For the rest of the day, we lived with a fearful expectation that later in the evening we were getting our mouths washed out with soap. It's never a pleasant experience to live with the fear of punishment when you've done something wrong.

The people who lived under the old system had a similar experience relating to God, only their experience offered little reprieve. It may seem strange to some people, but according to God, the only way to receive forgiveness is through the shedding of blood. Therefore, the people were required to perform animal sacrifices that provided a temporary covering of their sins. Since the blood of bulls and goats was insufficient to take away their sins completely, they were instructed to repeat the ritual year after year perpetually. As a result, the people lived under a constant reminder of their sin that did not allow them to escape the pestering fear of punishment.

God always had a plan to liberate the people from the condemnation of the law, which leads us to the third primary blessing of the new covenant known as *total forgiveness*. The prophet

Jeremiah continued the prophesy: "For I will forgive their wickedness and will remember their sins no more" (Jeremiah 31:34). Total forgiveness means that believers now live under a perpetual state of forgiveness—past, present, and future. In other words, we are not people who need to *get forgiven* every time we make a mistake. Instead, believers *are forgiven* based on the blood of Jesus that was shed on the cross.

Jesus's sacrifice was perfect, complete, and permanent, which means that no other blood sacrifice will ever be required. Since we can be forgiven only through the shedding of blood, we are now totally forgiven people and have been made perfect forever based on the effectiveness of the blood of Christ. The author of Hebrews said it this way, "But when this priest had offered for all time one sacrifice for sins, he sat down at the right hand of God, and since that time he waits for his enemies to be made his footstool. For by one sacrifice he has made *perfect forever* those who are being made holy" (Hebrews 10:12–14).

The Internal Process

One of the hallmarks of a successful company is the ability to create systems and processes that generate high-quality, repeatable, and predictable results. That is why you will receive the same experience at any Chick-fil-A restaurant across the country. It doesn't matter which location you choose or who is working behind the counter, you will always be served the same quantity and quality of food and enjoy the recipes you love. Even the layout of the restaurants and customer service experiences are the same across the board. This is made possible because the company has developed powerful processes that define how everything is done at each location. If the employees were asked to get the job done without clear processes, the results would be disastrous every time. At the end of the day, it's the quality of the process that empowers the workers to produce superior results.

We have limited understanding of what God is doing behind the scenes in our lives, which can give the appearance at times that He is somewhat spontaneous. Difficult circumstances can seem chaotic and out of control until God comes through at the last—perfect—moment. As a result, we might get the impression that we are provided no clear process for how we are designed to live on this side of the cross. However, God operates in a perfect structure and systematic way. Consider for a moment the order and design of the cosmos, human body, and central nervous system. It doesn't take much effort to realize that only a highly systemized mind could have put the universe together.

Regarding how we are designed to function on this side of the cross, God created a process that empowers everyday believers to produce exceptional results. In the same way that Chick-fil-A does not throw employees into the kitchen and demand results without a clear process, God does not demand spiritual results without giving believers a clear process that makes successful living possible. In short, the Lord has established a divine business process that works to produce extraordinary results through ordinary people. The key to the process is staying in alignment with its logical sequence; otherwise, the results will be disastrous. This may sound like another religious checklist but, instead, is the order of how God works in our lives.

Paul outlines the sequence in a letter written to the Ephesian church: "For it is by *grace* you have been saved, through *faith*—and this is not from yourselves, it is the gift of God—not by works, so that no one can boast. For we are God's handiwork, created in Christ Jesus to do good *works*, which God prepared in advance for us to do" (Ephesians 2:8–10). Notice the order of events that exists within the process. It starts with the blessing of *grace*, which is the divine power that makes victorious living possible. We must understand that it's only through the power of grace that believers can receive the spiritual substance of *faith*, which represents the second part of the sequence. Finally, we see the climax of the divine business process manifest when the believer exercises faith in the form of good *works*.

We often view grace as the act of overlooking faults or giving someone the benefit of the doubt. Believers have indeed received unmerited favor in this sense; however, the original use of the word *grace* also speaks to the idea of God *exerting holy influence* upon the human soul. In other words, believers are given the spiritual capacity to have faith only because God exerted holy influence in advance. For example, Peter did not muster up enough faith to walk on water on his own. Instead, he waited until Jesus gave him the verbal blessing to walk on water. It was through the words that Jesus spoke that gave Peter the confidence to step out of the boat. The process started with God exerting holy influence, which released the *grace* that Peter needed to have *faith*, which ultimately resulted in the extraordinary *work* of walking on water.

Mary, the mother of Jesus, had seen enough evidence over the years to know that whatever Jesus said, no matter how absurd it may seem, would produce miraculous results when His words were acted upon. We see her confidence in the holy influence of God when she told the disciples to "Do whatever he tells you" (John 2:5) midway through a wedding celebration when the hosts ran out of wine. Jesus told the servants to fill six stone jars with water and to draw out some for the master of the banquet. The servants had a decision to make. Would they believe that acting on the words of Jesus would produce miraculous results, or would they continue to operate based on human strength?

Their willingness to trust what Jesus said resulted in the water turning into wine. Again, we see the sequence of the divine business process in operation. It was the words that Jesus spoke that provided the *grace* the servants needed to step out on *faith*, which resulted in the *work* of turning water into wine. In the same way, we are called to live a supernatural life that far exceeds human ability, but without the power of grace, nothing will be made possible for the believer. Therefore, we must never attempt to change the proper sequence of events by putting works in front of the divine power of grace. Otherwise, we will find ourselves far removed from the victory we have been promised. Many people don't understand why they are constantly tired, frustrated, and burned out in their spiritual lives. I can tell you from personal experience that doing works that are out of sequence will never produce the intended results.

We were never designed to live the supernatural life separate from the divine power source of grace. Therefore, we must learn to walk in alignment with the grace of God if we want to live victoriously. Rest assured, we have been given a new way to live that takes the heavy burden off of our shoulders and places it on the very capable shoulders of God. Jesus said, "Come to me, all you who are weary and burdened, and I will give you rest. Take my yoke upon you and learn from me, for I am gentle and humble in heart, and you will find rest for your souls. For my yoke is easy and my burden is light" (Matthew 11:28–30).

The Tagline

Now that we've introduced the blessings of the new covenant and established the importance of grace, we can unveil the spiritual growth process I mentioned earlier in this chapter. As a reminder, when we were in the planning stages of launching Imagine Church, I intended to create a simple process that guards against the tendency to rely on human strength and maintains the brand integrity of the gospel. We have accomplished each of these goals while also placing the power of grace at the center of the equation. I have summarized the spiritual growth process using the following simple tagline: Be loved. Belong. Be you.

In the world of marketing, taglines are used to communicate the value of a brand and inspire people to take action. The most effective taglines are brief, memorable, and generate an emotional connection with the target audience. For example, in 1988 Nike debuted their former tagline Just Do It, which created enormous notoriety and success for the company. Although the phrase did not mention anything about shoes, sportwear, or athletics, it was highly effective at capturing the mind-set of most athletes.

My dad was an avid runner growing up and often toured the world with a bicycle group. One afternoon he returned home from a long run he frequently did around the neighborhood. He walked down the hallway and entered the family room where I was sitting on the couch watching television in the lazy man's position. At that exact moment, a motivating Nike advertisement was playing on the television that ended with the powerful tagline Just Do It. With sweat pouring down his face, my dad glanced over to where I was reclined and said, "I just did it." I can't deny that I felt inspired to get outside and start exercising myself. Touché, Dad! The point is that good taglines capture a company's brand essence and inspire consumers.

When it comes to the spiritual growth process for the church, what might appear as a catchy marketing phrase represents something far more significant. The process behind the tagline Be loved. Belong. Be you. offers you a path toward spiritual growth designed to liberate you from self-reliance, empower you to live victoriously, and release you to express God's love to the world. Each stage of the process upholds the brand integrity of the gospel and ensures the power of grace is the driving force. The process can be summarized as follows:

- *Be loved* is founded on the blessing of *total forgiveness* and empowers you to overflow with love in such a way that news about Jesus spreads to every part of the world.

- *Belong* is founded on the blessing of *intimate relationship* and guides you into dynamic life-giving relationships no matter where you are on your spiritual journey.

- *Be you* is founded on the blessing of *new creation* and releases you to express God's love to the world in your unique way.

We will spend the next three chapters breaking down the spiritual growth process and giving you the tools to succeed. I am convinced that everyone who embraces this new-covenant, grace-centered approach will find true spiritual freedom and attract more people to Jesus.

Chapter 7

Be Loved

We love because He first loved us.

JOHN THE APOSTLE

THE FIRST STEP OF the spiritual growth process is learning how to receive God's love. This thought may seem backward at first because we have been taught that loving God is our top priority. I have heard many sermons over the years that compel believers to strive harder to love God and love other people. In many ways, this sentiment has become the mantra of the modern church. I fully agree that love represents the most important expression in the believer's life, but I have not heard many people explain exactly how we are designed to love.

Before we go into detail about how love works, let's take a moment to consider the magnitude of what we have been asked to do. If you're anything like me, the idea of reflecting the love of God to the world is quite intimidating. It's one thing to love people we find easy to love. We can round up all the Care Bears in the world and give them a nice warm squeeze. However, the real problem is being asked to love people who are difficult to love. The person who hurt you growing up. The spouse who cheated on you. The neighbor who constantly makes your life difficult. The person you see in the mirror every morning. We are called to love everyone.

If loving everyone were not enough, consider that we are also called to model our love after Jesus. This is where things get complicated. Now we're talking about a depth of love that goes well beyond human capacity. It's one thing to have coffee with a friend who did you wrong, but Jesus offered the greatest form of love by dying on the cross. Words can't describe the moral strength required to love in this way. Jesus was tortured for hours and placed on the cross to die in humiliation. He looked down at the people who were executing Him and said, "Father, forgive them, for they do not know what they are doing" (Luke 23:34). Is there any person who can match the purity and strength of this love?

In my estimation, we have ourselves quite the dilemma. On the one hand, we are called to reflect a love that never fails, but on the other hand, we do not have the capacity to meet that standard. Where does this leave us? In his letter to the Galatians, Paul offers a glimpse into how we are designed to love on this side of the cross: "I have been crucified with Christ and I no longer live, but *Christ lives in me*. The life I now live in the body, I live by faith in the Son of God, who loved me and gave himself for me" (Galatians 2:20). In this one verse, Paul describes a new way to live that is no longer dependent on human ability. The old person we once were has been crucified with Christ and replaced with a new spiritual identity that is inseparable from Christ. Therefore, we are now in a position where *Christ lives in us and through us*. It's staggering to consider that we are no longer on our own, but it's Christ doing the living, and the loving, through us.

Paul did more to love people than I could ever imagine. You can see the extent he was willing to love by the persecution he endured: "I have worked much harder, been in prison more frequently, been flogged more severely, and been exposed to death again and again" (2 Corinthians 11:23). However, it's important to note that Paul did not consider any of these events possible without the power of grace living through him: "But by the grace of God I am what I am, and his grace to me was not without effect. No, I worked harder than all of them—yet not I, but the grace of God that was with me" (1 Corinthians 15:10). When it comes to how we are designed to live on this side of the cross, only the power of grace can take us beyond our human limitations to love.

The next time you feel stretched to love beyond your ability, keep in mind that you are not doing the loving alone. You may not have the strength to forgive the person who caused you serious harm, but the Christ who lives in you has the strength. You may not have the ability to serve the people in your community who gossip about you, but the Christ who lives in you has the ability. You may not have the capacity to lead your family, handle the ministry position, or endure the persecutions, but the Christ who lives in you has the capacity. As believers, we must recognize that we are not striving to match the greatness of Christ's love; instead, we are simply allowing Christ to love through us. He will lead you to love people in ways you never thought possible.

The New Command

As we peel back the layers even further, I want to challenge believers to uphold the brand integrity of the gospel regarding the topic of love. If we are going to stay true to the new covenant, we must challenge ourselves to rethink certain perspectives about spiritual growth. This is particularly true regarding one of the most prominent statements made by Jesus. When asked by a Jewish audience to identify the greatest commandment, Jesus paraphrased the entire law-based system into one powerful statement: "'Love the Lord your God with all your heart and with all your soul and with all your mind.' This is the first and greatest command. And the second is like it: 'Love your neighbor as yourself.' All the Law and the Prophets hang on these two commandments" (Matthew 22:37–40).

This statement shows that love was the true intention behind every requirement under the law. In the mind of God, it wasn't so much about keeping the rules so the people could avoid being cursed. Instead, love is a relational word, which means that God wanted the people to operate based on love, first with their Creator and then with other people. It's interesting to note that both the old and new covenants share the same goal of producing love. However, because the old system was only a shadow of the good things to come, love was limited to the ability of the people. Perhaps the most obvious difference between the old and new covenants is the process God uses to manifest love through people.

I want to draw your attention to the power source that Jesus referenced in the greatest commandment. The people were asked to love based on the strength of *their* hearts, the strength of *their* souls, and the strength of *their* minds. In other words, the entire system of the law was founded on the strength of the people to generate love. Perhaps some people could love better than others, but nobody could attain the highest standard of love shown by Jesus. It should come as no surprise the brand value of love is described as the fruit of Spirit, not the fruit of human strength.

I wonder how many well-meaning believers today base their entire approach to Christian living on the greatest commandment. How many church leaders create discipleship processes that are derived from this approach? How many people wake up every morning determined to love with all their heart, soul, and strength? The fastest way to disrupt the sequence of the divine business process is to put *works* in front of *grace*. However, Jesus's summary of the law was consistent with the limitations of the law-based system that relied on human strength. Therefore, we must not continue to base our lives on the summary of a system that has been replaced with something so much better.

If this teaching makes you feel uncomfortable because you want to honor the words of Jesus, please allow me to provide more context. I share your desire to honor the words of Jesus;

therefore, I urge you to consider the whole counsel of His words as we seek to uphold the brand integrity of the gospel. It's true that Jesus provided a summary of the law to the Jewish people under the law, but we can't overlook that He also provided a summary of the new covenant for people on this side of the cross. For reasons I can't fully explain, many believers continue to exalt the summary of the law-based system above the summary of the new system that is based on grace. It's my hope that a greater understanding of the new command will compel believers to rethink their approach to Christian living.

"A new command I give you: Love one another. As I have loved you, so you must love one another" (John 13:34). At first glance, this statement from Jesus might appear like the former commandment, but the fundamental differences are striking. The new command seeks to achieve the same objective of love, but it provides the power of grace that is needed to generate love through people. Notice that in the process of asking believers to love one another, Jesus prefaces the command with the offer to love them first: "*As I have loved you*, so you must love one another." In other words, on this side of the cross, believers are merely conduits of Christ's love. It's the process of first receiving love through an intimate relationship with Christ that we can truly reflect the quality of His love to others. The more we understand and experience God's love in our lives, the more love we have in our hearts to give to other people. The importance of the phrase *be loved* cannot be overstated.

My dad always made sure that he tucked us kids in every night before we went to sleep. It was our tradition to brush our teeth and then call him when we were in bed. However, being the only adopted child in the family, I did not automatically assume that I was loved. One night I decided to put my dad's love to the test by pretending that I was already asleep when he came downstairs. When he called to ask if we were ready to be tucked in, I didn't say anything. After a few minutes, he finally came into my room and placed his hand on my back. Believing that I was already fast asleep, my father quietly spoke a prayer over me, kissed me on the cheek, and whispered that he loved me. After he left the room, I could not stop the tears from pouring down my face. It was the first time I genuinely believed that my father loved me. To be clear, I am certain that he loved me from the moment I came to the family, but I had a difficult time believing I was loved. In the same way, God wants to remove the doubts that often prevent us from believing we are loved and accepted by our heavenly Father.

Grace and Truth

For the law was given through Moses;
grace and truth came through Jesus Christ.
John 1:17

In the process of learning how to be loved, we can all relate to the woman at the well. If you're not familiar with her story, the woman did everything she could to find love. We all have a void in our hearts that can be satisfied only with the love of God. As a result, we often search for love in all the wrong places only to find ourselves in an even worse condition. In the woman's case, she went from one sexual relationship to another, searching for a man who could make her feel loved. Unfortunately, in the process of living a promiscuous lifestyle, she had become an outcast among her people.

One day the woman traveled to the nearby well to get some water. Normally, women traveled together in groups, but the other ladies did not want her around. When she arrived at the location, it just so happened that Jesus was resting at the well after a long journey from Judea. It was customary for Jewish people to avoid any contact with Samaritans; however, Jesus broke every rule in the book by asking her for a drink of water. You can imagine the woman's surprise, "You are a Jew and I am a Samaritan woman. How can you ask me for a drink?" (John 4:9). Jesus did not allow the barriers of culture to prevent Him from extending love to the woman. The mere act of speaking to her would have affirmed that she had value in His eyes.

The woman sensed something unique about the interaction, but the encounter was about to get even more interesting. Jesus described a different type of water that would take away her thirst forever. He told her that this water would become like a spring that wells up into eternal life. Intrigued, the woman replied to Jesus, "Sir, give me this water so that I won't get thirsty and have to keep coming here to draw water" (John 4:15). Perhaps she thought Jesus was talking about a natural water source that would require less travel and work to access. However, Jesus wanted to give her a relationship that would permanently satisfy her desire to be loved. We can spend a lifetime drinking from the wrong well until we choose to finally receive God's love.

The woman had no reason to believe that Jesus knew anything about her past. However, the conversation quickly turned personal when she agreed to receive the water. Jesus said in response, "Go, call your husband and come back" (John 4:16). The woman replied that she did not have a husband, but Jesus did not settle for anything short of the truth concerning her lifestyle. God's love is best understood in the context of our most grievous failures. It's for this reason Jesus did the unthinkable by bringing her darkest secrets to the forefront: "You are right when you say you have no husband. The fact is, you have had five husbands, and the man you now have is not your husband. What you have said is quite true" (John 4:17–18). It may seem cruel to have embarrassed the woman in this way, but it requires honesty about our past to allow the power of grace to change our future.

At this point, the woman knew she was speaking to someone with divine insight. I imagine she rehearsed a familiar thought process in her mind: "Why is this man even bothering with me? I already know my life is a failure." When the truth about who we really are is exposed, we often feel a strong sense of unworthiness. You might feel unlovable because you are weighed down by secret sins in your life. You might have a track record of failures that prevents you from believing you are loved. However, it's important to understand that Jesus did not meet this woman by accident. The entire interaction was a divine setup from heaven to free her from the spiritual bondage of trying to fill the void in her heart through sexual relationships. It's why Jesus took the unprecedented step to reveal Himself as the promised Messiah to this woman, "I, the one speaking to you—I am he" (John 4:26). God used this woman to show that He will meet us right in the middle of our dirty messes and that He often chooses the most disreputable people to accomplish His purposes.

As you can imagine, the woman was moved by her interaction with Jesus. She quickly hurried back to the village without bothering to take her water jar. Listen very closely to the words she spoke to the people in her town, "Come, see a man who *told me everything I ever did*. Could this be the Messiah?" (John 4:29). Think about the unusual nature of her testimony for a moment. The woman was not excited about seeing blinded eyes healed or lepers made whole. Instead, she was enamored that Jesus told her everything she ever did wrong. Why would anybody feel blessed about a spiritual leader, maybe even the promised Messiah, exposing her dirty laundry in this way? The answer is simple. Despite knowing everything about her past, Jesus loved the woman most genuinely. When the ugly truth about who we really are encounters the living embodiment of grace, we will finally understand what it means to be loved.

You may be asking similar questions. "Could this be the Messiah? Is Jesus really willing to accept me right where I am and love me despite my past?" I am here to tell you that Jesus is that passionate about loving you. God has extended the offer of *total forgiveness* to anyone willing to receive His love. If you have already accepted Jesus as your personal Savior, have faith that His blood is powerful enough to keep you forgiven. If you have not accepted Jesus as your personal Savior, I invite you to receive the greatest offer of love that will ever be extended to you. You can know with certainty that God will meet you in the middle of your ugly truth.

Confident Love

Peter was an awesome disciple who walked on water and preached the sermon on Pentecost that resulted in three thousand souls being added to the church, but he also got himself into trouble from time to time. For example, when Jesus predicted that He was going die at the hands of the chief priests, Peter said there was no way he was going to let that happen. Of course, the cross represented the very purpose for why Jesus was born. Therefore, Jesus did not mince words in His response to Peter: "Get behind me, Satan! You are a stumbling block to me; you do not have in mind the concerns of God, but merely human concerns" (Matthew 16:23). This would qualify as one of those "ouch" moments in our walk with Christ.

Despite his flaws, Peter was the type of guy you would want in your corner during a street fight. When Jesus was arrested in the garden of Gethsemane, Peter drew his sword and cut off the ear of the high priest's servant. Unfortunately, however, it was his passion to defend his friends that also represented his greatest weakness. Peter would soon learn that his love for Jesus had its limitations and was not fully developed. Sometimes we must experience the sting of failure to understand the proper order of the divine business process. In this case, Peter's overconfidence in his ability to love was about to receive a painful spiritual readjustment.

Jesus warned the disciples that when the time came for Him to be crucified, each of them would abandon Him. This must have been tough for the disciples to hear, but it was prophesied many years prior that this is exactly what would happen. Jesus was destined to conquer the final enemy of death alone. However, Peter stood in strong opposition to the warning. "Even if all fall away on account of you, I never will" (Matthew 26:33).

The lack of awareness Peter had about himself at this moment is striking. Paul once said, "Do not think of yourself more highly than you ought, but rather think of yourself with sober judgment, in accordance with the faith God has distributed to each of you" (Romans 12:3).

Although he felt brave at the moment, Peter would soon learn that his love was not strong enough to withstand even the pressure of a humble servant girl. On the night that Jesus stood on trial with the Sanhedrin, the servant girl approached Peter and insisted that he was one of the disciples. This was followed by another girl and then several other people who made the same accusation. In each case, Peter vehemently denied knowing Jesus. "I don't know the man!" he pushed back (Matthew 26:72). After coming to the full realization that his resolve to love Jesus had failed miserably, Peter broke down in tears.

This must have been a tough lesson for Peter, but it also represented the start of an exciting new season. We must all reach the point in our lives where we understand that our ability to love God is not the basis of the gospel. Instead, the love within ourselves has been initiated, developed, and strengthen by God; therefore, we must place our confidence securely in the love of Christ. John the apostle said it best: "This is love: not that we loved God, but that He loved us and sent his Son as an atoning sacrifice for our sins" (1 John 4:10). The message of the gospel has always been God's love for humanity, not the other way around.

After the resurrection, Jesus took the time to restore Peter in front of the other disciples by asking, "Simon son of John, do you love me more than these?" (John 21:15). Peter responded to the question, "Yes, Lord, you know that I love you." Interestingly, the version of the word *love* that Jesus used in the original language was *agapas*, which speaks to the highest quality of love that comes from God. However, the version of the word *love* that Peter used in response was *philio*, which expresses a *reciprocal* type of love. In other words, Peter understood that his strength to love God going forward would be established first upon God's love for him.

Paul's Prayer

On May 28, 2015, I posted a message on Facebook that deserved a lot more likes than it received. I had spent my entire adult life serving in ministry but did not have total clarity on my calling. After years of learning, growing, and developing in the Lord, I finally reached the point where I knew exactly what I was called to do. For the record, I could have posted a picture of an ugly cat and received hundreds of likes, but instead I waxed poetic about my purpose in life and received five likes. Regardless, my post included this prayer from the apostle Paul that now represents the theme Scripture for my life: "*And I pray that you*, being rooted and established in love, may have power, together with all the Lord's holy people, to *grasp how wide and long and high and deep* is the love of Christ, and to know this love that surpasses knowledge—*that you may be filled* to the measure of all the fullness of God" (Ephesians 3:17–19).

This one short prayer represents the backdrop to the most important spiritual growth element in every believer's life. The prayer is located at the midway point of the letter to the Ephesians. In the first half of the letter, Paul focuses heavily on the incredible spiritual blessings we have received in Christ. He touches on concepts that theologians have searched out for hundreds of years, such as being chosen, blameless, adopted, loved, redeemed, forgiven, called—the list goes on. You might consider the first half of the letter a summary of the finished work of Christ. The spiritual blessings that have been lavished upon every believer are so profound, it's hard to wrap our minds around them. We will never fully comprehend the magnitude of what God has done for us.

Paul understood better than anyone that maintaining the proper sequence of the divine business process—*grace, faith,* and *works*—is paramount to how we are designed to live. In fact, the divine process was originally written in this same letter to the Ephesians. The significance of the prayer being located at the midway point of the letter highlights the importance of the divine process. Many people get stuck in their spiritual lives because there is too much emphasis on good works, which Paul describes in more detail toward the end of the letter. We are often bombarded with teachings that elevate the importance of avoiding sin, getting involved in the church, and doing a better job of loving people. However, when believers are not firmly rooted and grounded in God's love first, they will either feel perpetually guilty for not doing enough or work hard to do all kinds of good works but profit nothing in the process.

To say this another way, Paul did not start with an outline of the spiritual blessings and then leapfrog all the way to good works. Instead, he paused in the middle of the letter to express a prayer that was meant to empower believers to become rooted and established in love. You can sense the urgency in Paul's heart to prevent his readers from glossing over this important spiritual truth. Paul writes that we must become established in love through the process of grasping, or comprehending, the *width* and *length* and *height* and *depth* of Christ's love. In other words, we must spend considerable time getting to know deep within our hearts what God has done for us and how He truly feels about us. This can only happen as we develop not merely a theological knowledge about love but experiential knowledge of His love.

Paul closes the prayer with the promise that we will be filled with *all the fullness of God* as we continue the process of being loved. If you feel uncomfortable with the premise that receiving love takes priority over good works, herein lies the spiritual value of the growth process. As we are filled with all the fullness of God, we will have the divine power that is needed to keep the right motives and sustain meaningful good works. We are not seeking to reach a destination when it comes to receiving God's love; rather, we are on a spiritual journey that will continue for the remainder of our lives. In the process, we will not merely have an intellectual or emotional perspective about love, but we will intimately know the love of God and will be filled with all the fullness of God.

I invite every believer to join me in the process of becoming a recipient of God's love. We will no longer strive to love God and love other people based on the limitations of human ability. Instead, we will be filled with love so that we might overflow with the brand value of love and have something of genuine substance to give the world. We will lead other people in the process of being loved so they don't get stuck in the performance trap. We will learn how to slow down and marinate in God's love when we find ourselves running on the fumes of human ability. Most important, we will stay rooted and grounded in the love of Christ so that we might live free and attract more people to Jesus.

Chapter 8

BELONG

Though one may be overpowered, two can defend themselves.

KING SOLOMON

THE SECOND STEP OF the spiritual growth process is choosing to integrate our lives with other life-giving believers. God's plan from the beginning was to bring people together from all walks of life into one large spiritual family—the body of Christ, which is the church. Sharing our lives with other believers is foundational to how we are designed to live on this side of the cross. However, we live in a world that has grown increasingly isolated in recent years despite the advancement of social media. Isolation is the greatest enemy of spiritual growth and will always result in painful outcomes. Therefore, we must be intentional about integrating our lives into the local church.

The prospect of sharing our lives with other believers is not merely a good idea; it's how we are designed to live. We were all born with an intrinsic need to belong. The need is so powerful that in the absence of healthy connections, we will go to extreme lengths to feel accepted, no matter the cost. Young people will subject themselves to the dangers of gang life. Young ladies will give themselves to any loser who makes them feel special. Men will stop at the local bar on the way home from work. We could solve many problems in our lives through the process of being more intentional about creating Christ-centered relationships.

In the most extreme cases, when a healthy community is missing from an individual's life, it will often lead to some type of addiction. I am convinced that most substance and behavioral strongholds are the result of substituting the need for human connection with an alternative destructive remedy. As addicts become more isolated from healthy relationships, they will seek to fill the void in their hearts through escape and fantasy. It's by no accident the centerpiece of most recovery programs involves group meetings. The process of integrating people back into community provides the human connection that was formerly missing. Whereas isolation leads to the destruction of the human soul, belonging to a life-giving community leads to an abundant life.

Contrary to popular belief, the intrinsic need to belong is not the result of evolution but can be traced back to the origin of all human life. It's fascinating to consider that before anything was created—including the heavens, angels, galaxies, animals, or any other living being—God existed entirely alone. However, although no other beings existed, God was not actually alone. It's impossible to fully understand this concept, but we learn throughout Scripture that God is one in nature while also three coexisting and coeternal persons—God the Father, God the Son, and God the Holy Spirit. As a result, God did not merely invent the concept of community, but the divine nature of His being *is* community.

We see this mystery start to unfold in the first chapter of the Bible. Scripture does not seek to answer *how* we were created, but we have received amazing insights into *why* we were created. In the following verse, we are given the opportunity to read the transcript from a heavenly board meeting that took place before humans were created. "Then God said, 'Let *us* make mankind in *our* image, in *our* likeness'" (Genesis 1:26).

In the process of articulating the intention to create mankind, God used the first-person pronouns *us* and *our* to identify the pluralistic nature of His being. In other words, one God existed in three persons in attendance at the board meeting. This glimpse into the mind of God offers powerful context to what being created in the image, or likeness, of God means. The reason we can think rationally is because we come from a rational God. The reason we feel guilty for doing wrong is because we come from a moral God. Finally, the reason we have an intrinsic need to belong is because we come from a pluralistic God. Therefore, since the human soul can thrive only in the context of community, God has established three primary relational categories to meet our need to belong and destroy the enemy of isolation: intimate relationship with God, marriage and the family unit, and Christ-centered gatherings.

Intimate Relationship with God

The first and most important relational category is having an *intimate relationship* with our heavenly Father. Like the woman at the well, we all have a thirst to belong that can be eternally quenched only when our spirits are connected to the source of all human life. The psalmist offers a poetic description of how the human soul is incomplete in the absence of God. "As the deer pants for streams of water, so my soul pants for you, my God. My soul thirsts for God, for the living God" (Psalm 42:1–2). Salvation represents the divine process that perfectly unites the human spirit with Christ and, as a result, removes our cosmic sense of loneliness. When it comes to being united with someone, we often think in terms of having a kindred spirit or sharing common interests. However, the reality of being perfectly united with Christ means that every possible barrier of separation has been eternally removed.

The better we understand the depth of God's love, the more we can heal our souls and find true inner peace. You may have been rejected by your natural father or have a track record of broken relationships. It could be that nobody else in the world wants to associate with you. However, despite what other people may have done to you or how you feel about yourself, the blessing of being accepted in Christ is based solely on the power of His love. Jesus's death on the cross paved the way for the relational chasm that existed between God and humanity to be reconciled. As a result, those who believe in Jesus have received the unspeakable blessing of becoming children of God: "Yet to all who did receive him, to those who believed in his name, he gave the right to become children of God—children born not of natural descent, nor of human decision or a husband's will, but born of God" (John 1:12–13).

The adoption we have received in Christ gives every believer instant status as a child of God, but it can take time to fully internalize our sense of belonging. It's for this reason the Holy Spirit works deep within our souls to speak words of affirmation concerning our relationship with God. Paul said it this way: "Because you are His sons, God sent the Spirit of his Son into our hearts, the *Spirit who calls out*, 'Abba, Father'" (Galatians 4:6). We must look closely at this verse to appreciate the true heart of the Father. The term *abba* in the original language was used to express the tender endearment of a child toward the father. However, in this verse, we see a beautiful reversal whereby the Spirit, not the child, calls out, "Abba, Father." In other words, our heavenly Father speaks to every insecurity in our souls until the true relational power of what it means to belong to God is fully known and experienced.

Marriage and the Family Unit

An intimate relationship with our heavenly Father is indeed paramount, but God also created human relationships to destroy the enemy of isolation. Specifically, we see that God was intentional about establishing *marriage and the family unit* as the human foundation to meet our relational needs. After creating the universe and breathing life into the first male human, the Lord said, "It is not good for the man to be alone. I will make a helper suitable for him" (Genesis 2:18). I'm sure that Adam was having a great time hanging out with the animals, but he needed more to feel connected and to accomplish his divine purpose. Therefore, God caused the man to fall into a deep sleep. Then He created the first woman out of the man's body. Adam now had a true companion to enjoy marriage, raise children, and live an abundant life.

The relational foundation of marriage provided the basis for God to bless Adam and Eve and release them to fulfill their divine destiny: "God blessed them and said to them, 'Be fruitful and increase in number; fill the earth and subdue it. Rule over the fish in the sea and the birds in the sky and over every living creature that moves on the ground'" (Genesis 1:28).

We have been given the freedom to multiply in numbers through traditional marriage and take dominion over the affairs of the earth. For some people, this means getting married and having children. Others, like the apostle Paul, choose to remain single to keep focused on serving God. It should come as no surprise that societies built upon the traditional family unit, the way it was designed by God, produce the most stable, healthy, and well-rounded people. However, the spirit of the antichrist has a deep hatred for anything that God has blessed. Many secular movements want to undermine the traditional family in every possible way. Therefore, as believers, we must not allow secular philosophies that stand in opposition to God's design for marriage and the traditional family to influence what we believe and how we live.

Christ-Centered Gatherings

God has drawn people together from every corner of the earth to dwell among His own people in the context of *Christ-centered gatherings.* Herein lies the challenge for many believers in modern society. We have been conditioned to promote family time and personal activities above everything else. However, many fail to recognize that going to church and doing life together with other believers is what makes marriages, children, and the traditional family unit that much stronger. To grow spiritually and walk in our divine destinies, we must not underestimate the importance of integrating into the local church.

One of the most rewarding aspects of being a pastor is watching broken people find healing through the process of integration. I have seen people start attending church after being released from prison and transform into powerful ministers of the gospel. However, perhaps the most difficult part of being a pastor is seeing people fall back into the trap of isolation. Separating ourselves from our spiritual families will always diminish the strength we need to walk in victory. In the same way that a lion seeks to isolate its prey from the pack before going in for the kill, Satan is watching for believers who isolate themselves from the church: "Your enemy the devil prowls around like a roaring lion looking for someone to devour" (1 Peter 5:8).

If you are not convinced that Satan wants to keep you away from church, consider what happened during the global pandemic that started in the year 2019. The health crisis created an even greater spiritual pandemic with implications that could last for decades. In the process of wanting to stay physically healthy and protect our loved ones, which should be an important consideration, many went down the path of permanently separating themselves from their spiritual communities. No matter where you stand concerning the pandemic, believers cannot overlook the many ways that Satan has exploited the crisis to create fear, isolation, and division. For example, I believe it was an act of spiritual treason to exalt the importance of casinos and liquor stores above the essential need to attend church. The local church should never be classified as nonessential, especially during a crisis when spiritual strength is needed the most.

I am deeply concerned that many believers have grown too comfortable not integrating back into their faith communities. Others have developed a misguided doctrine that suggests in-person gatherings are not important anymore due to the advancement of digital technology. At Imagine Church, we have created a digital church experience, but we use the platform to reach new people and to provide an alternative way to engage with those who can't attend church in person. However, we must never view digital church "attendance" as a comparable alternative to in-person meetings. Isolation from real human connections will always lead to spiritual apathy and result in the resurfacing of unhealthy coping mechanisms.

Christ-centered gatherings are designed to produce explosive spiritual results that can't be replicated in any other format. I love spending time alone praying, watching a message online, and enjoying the presence of God. However, the spiritual dynamics that happen during an in-person gathering have a far greater impact. It's in these environments the Lord makes His presence known and the angels celebrate together with God's people. While growing up, you may have been dragged to church services that put you to sleep, but you need to give this church thing another chance. God is the most exciting person you will ever know and wants to release fresh measures of faith, hope, and love into your spirit. If you have attended churches that feel dead, stuffy, and boring, God has more for you in a church that has developed a faith-filled, life-giving culture.

The value of corporate gatherings also extends to the relational aspects that happen in church. For example, you will never get the same experience watching a movie on your laptop as going to a packed movie theater. Reciprocal energy happens within a church gathering that is contagious. As people lift their hands in response to the promptings of the Holy Spirit, others are inspired to also receive from God. Healing takes place as we raise our voices together in adoration to the Lord. Our faith is strengthened when other people affirm what we know is true in the Bible. Not to mention the opportunity to serve people and learn from gifted teachers. There is nothing like going to church and greeting each other with a big smile, warm hug, and a "God bless you!"

True Integration

It's been said that blood is thicker than water, but spirit is even thicker than blood. We all need the support that comes from blood relatives. However, the value of our spiritual families has even greater worth. Those who do not have a relationship with Christ can provide no spiritual support to the believer. Even unbelieving relatives with the best intentions will lead us astray regarding matters of faith. We should never forsake our relatives or dishonor them in any way, but the process of true integration begins with the understanding that we also belong to a larger spiritual family. Jesus once pointed to His disciples and said, "Here are my mother and my brothers. For whoever does the will of My Father in heaven is My brother and sister and mother" (Matthew 12:49–50). Believers offer the most powerful spiritual support network available among people.

However, it's possible to visit the same church for many years yet remain isolated from the available spiritual support. We must understand that attending church is only the first step toward making life-long friends who can add spiritual texture to our journeys. Therefore, one of the strategies we use at Imagine Church to help believers move toward true integration is the opportunity to participate in small groups. The writer of Hebrews lays the foundation for how small group meetings can provide amazing spiritual benefits: "And let us consider how we may spur one another on toward *love and good deeds*, not giving up meeting together, as some are in the habit of doing, but encouraging one another—and all the more as you see the Day approaching" (Hebrews 10:24–25).

The writer encourages the continuation of in-person gatherings so that believers might spur one another toward *love and good deeds*. This provides another layer of spiritual value that occurs particularly well in small groups. The time spent together in more intimate settings creates the opportunity for believers to serve one another through prayer, encouragement, and hospitality, helping us to develop our spiritual gifts while providing an outlet for ministry that is not available during weekend services. In addition, small groups cultivate the safe space that is needed to share what's going on in our lives. This opens the door for believers to receive timely words and practical support from their friends.

At Imagine Church, one woman regularly attended our weekend services who always seemed to be in a bad mood. There were times she avoided everyone in the church and even came across as angry. It was clear that something was not right in her life. When we first launched the small group model, I was pleased to learn that she joined one of the groups. After a few weeks, I noticed a remarkable change was taking shape with her countenance. The woman came to church with a smile on her face and a new bounce in her step. Her small group leader told me that during one of the meetings, she broke down in tears while the other people in the group gathered around her to pray. I don't know any of the other details that happened that night, but, clearly, the woman received spiritual deliverance.

It must have been only six months later, the same woman unexpectedly died from a brain disease. I had the privilege of speaking at her memorial service and shared the testimony about how her life was changed a few months prior. Nobody could deny that God orchestrated the timing of what happened in the small group. As a result, we all had peace of mind knowing the woman was safely in the arms of Jesus. This was not the result of a dynamic church service with great music and a charismatic speaker. Instead, God used a home group to bring spiritual deliverance in her life only months before she passed away. True integration always starts with an awareness of the incredible spiritual value that it provides.

Church Hurts

When you hang around church long enough, you will begin to see certain patterns take place that prevent believers from growing spiritually. The process of integrating our lives with other people is no small proposition. Things always get messy when multiple people are involved, and it requires true spiritual grit to come out better on the other side. Unfortunately, it's often within the messy context of integration that Satan creates division and isolates people from their spiritual strength. The Enemy knows that it takes time for believers to grow where they have been planted; therefore, he uses the spirit of offense to generate conflicts and cause people to turn against one another and ultimately leave the church.

The process typically begins when one person gets offended by another person in the church. It's worth noting that in most cases, both parties have some share in the blame. However, whether the grievance was legitimate or it was an honest misunderstanding, the opportunity for the Enemy to create isolation has now surfaced. As the spirit of offense festers long enough in the person's heart, the Enemy stirs things up until the person shares the offense with other people in the church. This is where the danger of the untamed tongue can set an entire forest ablaze. Now more people are offended, and the gossip spreads even deeper in the church. The spirit of offense will always find the most vulnerable people who lack the spiritual fortitude to protect the church. It's for this reason Jesus instructed believers to handle their grievances quickly and between only the two parties involved.

One consistent theme exists in every church hurt we might experience—ourselves. It could be that when more than one church relationship ends poorly, God is trying to get our attention that we are the ones who need to grow spiritually. God does have an appointed time for a person to leave a church, but most people leave churches for petty reasons. Therefore, we must desire to grow in our faith more than we desire to avoid the awkward process of growth. Scripture paints a beautiful picture of what happens when a person chooses to grow where they have been planted: "The righteous will flourish like a palm tree, they will grow like a cedar of Lebanon; *planted in the house of the Lord,* they will flourish in the courts of our God" (Psalm 92:12–13).

I started going to church at the age of twenty-one while attending the University of Washington. It was a small church that was started by people I knew were trustworthy in the Lord. I subsequently stayed in the same church for the next seventeen years. During that time, I was blessed with this family of believers to share victories and encourage one another when life was tough. There were also seasons when my lack of maturity made life and relationships harder for me. It would have been much easier in the short term to leave during those seasons, but it was only through the process of staying the course that I was able to learn some important lessons and grow in character. To promote spiritual growth, Paul challenges believers to overcome the schemes of Satan by having a shared commitment to love one another even through difficult conflicts: "*Bear with each other* and forgive one another if any of you has a grievance against someone. Forgive as the Lord forgave you. And over all these virtues put on love, which *binds them all together* in perfect unity" (Colossians 3:13–14).

We must understand that the only way to belong within a church family is to bear with one another regarding our respective character flaws. Notice that love functions as the *binding adhesive* that allows people within a spiritual community to operate in perfect unity. I needed constant grace from my spiritual leaders to work through my pride, immaturity, and development issues. There were also times when I was required to bear under the flaws of other people. We often think of love as an emotion, but true love is made from the ingredients of blood, patience, and sacrifice. It's only within the context of community we can learn how to share the love we have received from Jesus. Therefore, the process of true integration causes a believer either to grow spiritually or leave prematurely.

I Don't Belong

I understand the emotional barriers that stand in the way of going to church. Some people feel they have been burned by church leaders and don't want to try again. Others are fully aware of their past mistakes and feel unworthy. Some say they practice their faith in other ways, or can't find a good church, or don't feel welcome at church. Aligning ourselves with God's plan for community requires that we push through every excuse and awkward phase we all face at times. As we set aside the barriers that have kept us in spiritual isolation, we will receive the blessings that await us on the other side.

Many years ago, a woman with an issue of blood decided to press into the community despite every good reason to stay home. She had spent all of her money going from one doctor to another, searching for a cure without any success. To make matters worse, the law-based system made the woman an outcast among her people. According to the law, any person with an issue of blood was considered unclean and was not allowed to touch other people until the bleeding stopped. Unfortunately, the monthly cycle that was normal for most women continued for twelve long years with this woman. As a result, she was not allowed to enter the local temple or even feel the warm embrace of a loved one. In short, the woman represented the living embodiment of what isolation does to the human spirit—she was emotionally broken, financially bankrupt, physically sick, and spiritually unclean.

One day Jesus was passing through a crowded area to heal the daughter of an important synagogue leader. The woman heard reports that Jesus was a miracle worker and knew that this was her only opportunity to get healed. However, the proposition required a great deal of risk. She would have to brush past many people in the crowd and openly break the law by touching Jesus. The woman tried to avoid being seen by approaching Jesus from behind and touching the edge of His clothes. Perhaps she wore a hooded garment to conceal her identity. In the same way, many people avoid going to church because they don't want their hidden issues exposed. Others come to church on occasion but sit in the back and leave quickly enough to prevent being seen.

Although the woman feared being exposed for having an issue of blood, it was her awareness that Jesus was her only hope that motivated her to push through the emotional discomfort that could have kept her in isolation. We learn that when she touched Jesus's clothing, the bleeding instantly stopped, and her sickness was completely healed. At this point, although she must have felt elated that her ailment was removed, you can imagine that she wanted to leave the area as quickly as possible to avoid being seen. Based on the statutes of the law-based system, the woman did not belong in the crowd. However, Jesus ruined her plans by turning around to address the people. "Who touched my clothes?" (Mark 5:30). This must have been the absolute worst-case scenario in the woman's mind. Knowing that she could not hide any longer, trembling with fear, she fell at the feet of Jesus and told Him the whole truth.

We all have issues in our life that could make us think that we don't belong at church. However, we learn from the woman that trusting God's plan will never leave us disappointed. In response to the woman's courage, Jesus said to her, "*Daughter*, your faith has healed you. Go in peace and *be freed* from your suffering" (Mark 5:34). Like the woman, many people have heard reports that Jesus can work miracles, but they have not heard that He wants to heal each of them from spiritual isolation. It was through the power of one spoken word to the woman, *daughter*, that lovingly affirmed her status as a child of God. Many people come to church expecting to receive a tongue-lashing from the all-knowing God, only to find themselves showered with acceptance from a loving Father.

However, there was more to the story that Jesus wanted to give the woman. It was her issue of blood that made her unclean according to the Jewish traditions, which meant that nobody wanted to be around her. You might feel that nobody wants to be around you. If that's the case, what's the point of even trying to integrate? However, Jesus did the work of bringing the woman publicly forward so that everyone could see that she was healed from the issue of blood and accepted by the Messiah. This gave the woman full permission to integrate back with her spiritual family, and it paved the way for the people to receive her with open arms. In the same way, God pours out His love into the hearts of every believer. You will be pleased to learn that people in healthy churches genuinely care and want to know you. Like the woman with the issue of blood, if you are willing to press through the awkward stage of true integration, you will receive the blessings of spiritual community that await you on the other side.

Chapter 9

BE YOU

Let your light shine before others, that they may see your good deeds and glorify your Father in heaven.

JESUS THE CHRIST

THE FINAL STEP OF the spiritual growth process is learning how to express God's love to the world in your unique way. The phrase *be you* represents the grand finale of what God wants to accomplish in our lives. We were each created for a specific purpose and are called to have a positive impact on the world. The *new creation* blessing represents the spiritual birth that makes the believer a new person in Christ. As a result, our new spiritual identity exists in perfect union with Christ, and we are qualified and empowered to live productive lives.

We have already outlined the importance of receiving God's love and integrating into the local church. As the light of the world, the process of spiritual growth should ultimately express God's love to the world through the manifestation of *good works*. A life that does not find its purpose in serving other people will always lack a sense of meaning. However, those who develop their spiritual gifts and embrace their true mission will have the most rewarding lives. Paul addresses the subject of good works in his letter to the Ephesians: "For we are his *workmanship*, created in Christ Jesus for *good works*, which God prepared beforehand, that we *should walk in them*" (Ephesians 2:10).

Every believer represents a living masterpiece who has been carefully put together to accomplish a specific purpose. In the same way that a master artist takes great care in selecting the right canvas for a painting, God takes great care in selecting each believer for a specific assignment. As a result, nothing about our lives happens outside of His sovereignty. Like the master artist, every stroke of the brush and color variance has been intricately applied to the canvas to prepare us for good works. The details that make us unique individuals, such as skin color, tone of voice, and personality, combined with the complex series of events that define our lives, shape us into the people we are today. You don't need to become someone else to live out your divine purpose—you just need to *be you*.

Paul reminds us that good works are not merely good ideas; they represent what we *should walk in* as we grow in our faith. At some point in the spiritual growth process, we are called to move past the consumer stage and share in the activity of building the church. If we can grow past our egos, agendas, and offenses, we can participate in the most significant work on the planet. Nothing is more rewarding than seeing people get saved and grow into vibrant believers. Paul reminds us in his farewell remarks to the Ephesians to apply the words of Jesus to our lives: "In everything I did, I showed you that by this kind of *hard work* we must help the weak, remembering the words the Lord Jesus himself said: 'It is more blessed to give than to receive'" (Acts 20:35).

Moving toward our divine purpose starts with the discovery of our spiritual gifts. Gaining more clarity about how we are designed to serve will dramatically impact our thoughts, decisions, and direction in life. After the prophet Samuel informed David that he was next in line to become king of Israel, David began to walk out his purpose in a greater way. In the process, everyone could see that he was a skilled musician, mighty warrior, and fearless leader. David was graced with the necessary gifts to accomplish his assignment. In the same way, the opportunity to discover our spiritual gifts will present itself as we take the time to serve in the church. Paul assures us that every believer has received at least one gift issued by the Spirit of God: "All these are the work of one and the same Spirit, and he distributes them to each one, just as he determines" (1 Corinthians 12:11).

The next step to producing good works is having a clear sense of direction for our lives. God is the ultimate visionary and knows how to place dreams in our hearts that bring out our best. As we continue to stay planted in the local church and get involved, we will develop a greater sense of clarity about our assignments. However, we will have to overcome a few common setbacks that prevent people from moving forward. For example, it's easy to feel unqualified to serve in the church because of past mistakes. Or we may have tried to step out on a dream in the past that didn't work out. Now is the time to release every negative thought that holds us back and embrace a new way of thinking. God used the prophet Isaiah to encourage the children of Israel, who, after being in exile for many years, did not believe they had a blessed future: "*Forget* the former things; do not dwell on the past. *See*, I am doing a new thing! Now it springs up; do you not perceive it? I am *making a way* in the wilderness and streams in the wasteland" (Isaiah 43:18–19).

The dreaming process always begins with the decision to *forget the former things*. We cannot move into the future if we're still looking in the rearview mirror. You may have tried to step out on faith in the past and your dreams didn't work out. Maybe your business failed or the ministry didn't get off the ground. It could be that you struggled with an addiction or had a moral failure and believe that you are washed-up goods at this point. Many kinds of "former things" have the potential to prevent us from believing that our lives still have a purpose. However, God wants us to understand that despite our past failures, He still has a plan for our future. The path to finding our sense of direction for the future starts with the decision to forget the former things.

Next, we must learn how to *perceive* where God is taking us, even when our lives don't seem prosperous at the moment. We may not see the full manifestation of our purpose right now, but God will cause circumstances to *spring up*, which offer clues to guide us forward. It could be that a door unexpectedly opens. Or perhaps a door closes that you thought would stay open. It's not our place to know every detail about the future, but we must perceive the next step in the journey. In some cases, God has already given us instructions and is waiting for us to make the next move. King Solomon reminds us that although we may have many ideas in our hearts, we will find the most success when we perceive what He desires for our lives: "Many are the plans in a person's heart, but it is the Lord's purpose that prevails" (Proverbs 19:21).

Finally, it's important to trust that God is *making a way* into the unknown places that we can't handle on our own. If we have a dream that could happen without any assistance from God, then the dream did not come from God. The prospect of walking into our destiny should feel slightly overwhelming, or perhaps even impossible, without help from above. If we limit our future to what we can handle on our own, we will not step into the deeper things that God is doing. It's easy to focus on the unknown variables that make us feel unqualified, but that's why we are in partnership with God. He will make a way in the *wilderness* where there is no clear path and provide streams in the *wasteland* when there are no resources.

As you consider using your spiritual gifts in the local church, it's important to note that doing good works does not begin with the full maturity of a dream. God takes us on a slow journey that prepares us for each new level of responsibility. For this reason, we must not despise the day of humble beginnings. I have worked with many aspiring believers who wanted to accomplish great things for the kingdom. However, doing great things always starts with a willingness to serve in small ways. If we get discouraged during the process of spiritual maturity, or don't have the patience to stay the course, we are subject to prematurely giving up on our dreams. So we must recognize that our purpose is not found in a destination; it's found in the person of Jesus Christ alone. We can take the next step in the journey knowing that we have already found our purpose being in relationship with Him.

License to Sin

I mentioned earlier in the book that some people continue to trust in rule keeping for daily living. We love to grip the handles of religion because it makes us feel more in control of our lives. Therefore, the prospect of no longer being under the law often provokes a few common objections: *Doesn't this give people a license to sin? How am I supposed to live without rules, laws, and moral codes?* The short answer is that believers are empowered to live on this side of the cross based on the new creation blessing, not rules written on paper. Paul reminds us that we now have the righteousness of Christ written on our hearts: "You show that you are a letter from Christ, the result of our ministry, written not with ink but the Spirit of the living God, not on tablets of stone but on tablets of human hearts" (2 Corinthians 3:3).

The *license-to-sin* objection is based on the premise that living under grace opens the door for sin to increase. I share in the desire to promote holy living, but we must not lack appreciation for the finished work of Christ in the process. The sequence of the divine business process is always based on grace alone through faith alone in the person of Jesus Christ. As a result, there is no basis for believers to take credit either for their salvation or for the security of their salvation. Paul addresses this issue in his letter to the Galatians: "Are you so foolish? After beginning by means of the Spirit, are you now trying to finish by means of the flesh?" (Galatians 3:3). In the same way that a believer is saved through faith in Christ alone, the believer must live through faith in Christ alone.

However, the real crux of the license-to-sin argument is purely hypothetical because it does not take into consideration the ramifications of the new creation blessing. If the believer has received a new spiritual identity that is congruent with the righteousness of Christ, why would we assume that believers want to sin? Paul follows this same logic in his letter to the Romans: "What shall we say, then? Shall we go on sinning so that grace may increase? By no means! We are those who have *died to sin*; how can we live in it any longer?" (Romans 6:1–2). The prospect of being *dead to sin* is not an aspirational concept; it's the current reality of every believer. As a result, when temptation knocks on the door, we must believe that we don't want to sin, that we detest everything sin represents, and that we will regret caving into sin. In short, we must agree that sin does not match our true spiritual identity anymore because we are *dead to sin*.

Paul continued his response to the license-to-sin argument with the suggestion that some people *do not know* the significance of the new creation blessing. "Or *don't you know* that all of us who were baptized into Christ Jesus were *baptized* into his death?" (Romans 6:3). Paul uses the symbolism of water baptism to offer a complete picture of the death, burial, and resurrection of Christ. As we take into consideration the full spectrum of salvation, we can place more confidence in the finished work of Christ. The act of submersion into the water represents the death of Christ that brings forgiveness of sins. Being under the water points to the burial of Christ, where the fallen condition of humanity is laid to rest forever. The final step of coming up out of the water symbolizes the resurrection of Christ, which means that we have been raised together with Christ as glorious new creations.

It would have been gracious enough to offer total forgiveness alone, but God wanted to provide His children with a new way to live that comes from the heart. Therefore, the old person was crucified with Christ and remains in the tomb, never to be seen again. In exchange, we have received a new heart that wants to please God and a born-again spirit that exists in perfect union with the Spirit of Christ. Although we may not always think, feel, or act as the new person, we must hold fast to the reality that we are righteous at the core. The more we believe that we are righteous, the more our actions will align with our new spiritual identity. Peter reminds us that those who do not grow in the fruit of the Spirit have *forgotten* who they are in Christ, "But whoever does not have them [fruit of the Spirit] is nearsighted and blind, *forgetting* that they have been cleansed from their past sins" (2 Peter 1:9).

We Are All Slaves

If there was anybody who understood the power of grace, it was the apostle Paul. He was doing quite well trusting in the strength of his own ability. He was circumcised on the eighth day, a strict follower of the law, and the most formidable persecutor of the first-century church. Every aspect of his attitudes, motives, and behaviors was self-serving and contrary to the righteousness of Christ. However, one day, despite his insatiable passion to fight against Christ, Paul was miraculously saved by the grace of God. Instantly, without any effort on his part, he was knocked to the ground and made a completely new creation.

Paul went from being the most feared persecutor of the church to its greatest advocate virtually overnight. It wasn't easy for the first-century Christians to believe that Paul, their most feared enemy, had suddenly become their most trusted ally. However, the change that Paul experienced was so genuine, over time the people learned to trust him because his lifestyle verified that his faith was sincere.

How does a person go from one lifestyle extreme to the other in such a dramatic fashion? It's not easy to think about slavery as a good thing, but when a person is saved, the Bible reveals he is taken from one form of slavery to another. Paul introduces this concept in his letter to the Romans. "When you were *slaves to sin*, you were free from the *control of righteousness*" (Romans 6:20). We may have fancied ourselves good people before we were saved, but we were owned by a tyrannical slaveowner called sin. As a result, we were alienated from the life of God and depraved from any form of righteousness. At the point of salvation, however, we were immediately transferred to a different slave owner, who put us under the *control of righteousness*. Under the first slaveowner, we could not stop sinning, but under the second slaveowner, we cannot keep sinning.

The concept of slavery underscores that believers go against their new identity when they choose to sin. We may indulge in the pleasures of sin for a moment but will soon experience the bitter cup of what it means to violate our righteousness in Christ. We will find ourselves navigating through the painful swamp of uncertainty, emptiness, and sorrow. The spirit of the believer exists in perfect union with the Spirit of Christ. Therefore, when we act in ways that go against our new identity, we feel the discomfort of a grieved Spirit. This experience lines up with Paul's reminder that we are now under the control of righteousness as *slaves to God*. "But now you have been set free from sin and have become *slaves of God*, the benefit you reap *leads to holiness*, and the result is eternal life" (Romans 6:22).

The new creation blessing is so powerful that it produces a change that lasts forever. The apostle John gives believers assurance that we will never revert to the identity of the old person: "No one born of God will continue to sin, because God's seed remains in them; they *cannot go on sinning*, because they have been born of God" (1 John 3:9). The idea that a believer *cannot go on sinning* may seem like a radical statement, but how could there possibly be any other outcome? The new birth does not merely represent a decision to live a better life; it involves the Spirit of God taking residence in the human heart. Therefore, the believer *cannot go on sinning* because the Word of God endures in our hearts forever. The apostle Peter further confirms that our new life in Christ can never be corrupted. "For you have been born again, not of perishable seed, but of *imperishable*, through the living and *enduring word of God*" (1 Peter 1:23).

Why We Still Sin

You may be reading this and wondering why you still sin. After all, if the believer has a new identity that no longer wants to sin, why do we still sin? I share in your desire to find answers to this pressing question. The idea that we cannot go on sinning does not suggest that we can reach sinless perfection in our daily actions. Although the work that took place at salvation produced a radically changed life, we know that every believer still has moments of failure. The reason we struggle at times is because we are battling forces that exist outside of our new spiritual identity that influence sin, namely, the *power of sin*, the *flesh*, and *Satan*. Although these forces can weave their way into our souls and give the illusion of being part of our new identity, they are independent of who we are in Christ.

We glimpse into the *power of sin* when Cain murdered his younger brother. The Lord warned Cain that he was in danger of succumbing to a force that wanted him to fail. "If you do what is right, will you not be accepted? But if you do not do what is right, *sin is crouching at the door; it desires to have you*, but you must rule over it" (Genesis 4:7). Here we see the power of sin is likened to a dangerous animal waiting to pounce on its prey. Although anger had been mounting in Cain's heart for some time, the power of sin was operating with its own *desire to have* control over his life. We live in a fallen world that is far removed from the environment that God originally created. Therefore, an unseen force exists: the power of sin that seeks to influence our thoughts, feelings, and actions.

The believer also must contend with the *flesh* regarding the issue of sin. The word *flesh* is translated from the Greek word *sarx*, which describes a carnal mind-set that is contrary to the Spirit of God. The idea of flesh does not suggest that we have two dueling natures, as many people believe, nor does it indicate that our bodies are unholy. We understand that the old self was crucified and we are now one new person in Christ. We also know that our bodies are the temple of the living God and should not be regarded as unholy. Instead, the flesh represents the thoughts, philosophies, and coping mechanisms that defined our lives prior to salvation. Although our spirits were made perfect at salvation, we retained certain carnal thought patterns that influence our actions. Paul admonishes believers to renew their minds to avoid reverting to old thinking patterns: "Do not conform to the pattern of this world, but be transformed by the renewing of your mind" (Romans 12:2).

Finally, we must contend with Satan and his demons when it comes to the issue of sin. The Enemy is always seeking to tempt people to sin against God based on three primary categories: the *lust of the flesh*, the *lust of the eyes*, and the *pride of life*. There is nothing wrong with getting angry or having a sex drive, but the Enemy will often appeal to our five senses when we are in a vulnerable state. This is what we call the *lust of the flesh*. Next, the Enemy also knows how to tantalize the *lust of the eyes* by showing us things that we should not covet, such as the fancy new sports car or items that belong to other people. The *pride of life* is how the Enemy tempts us to inflate our egos and prop ourselves above other people. The apostle John reminds us that every way the Enemy tempts believers will not satisfy our lives and is limited to the temporal pleasures of the world. "For everything in the world—the *lust of the flesh*, the *lust of the eyes*, and the *pride of life*—comes not from the Father but from the world" (1 John 2:16).

A New Way to Live

I promised earlier in the book to answer the question, how are we supposed to live without rules, laws, and moral codes? We have indeed received a new way to live that does not involve the law. However, the concept of being under grace is still foreign to many people who are dogmatic about legalism or have grown accustomed to reliance on the law. I once spoke with an aspiring young minister who clung to law-based living with all his might.

I tried to explain the blessings we have received on this side of the cross. However, the young man doubled down on his law-based approach anyway. "I wake up every day and try with all of my strength to follow the law and not sin." I am writing to those who have grown tired, burdened, and frustrated with the spiritual burnout that happens when we trust in our strength.

The new way we are designed to live elevates the believer into victorious living based on the power of grace. In the same way the law of aerodynamics lifts the eagle high above the earth by overriding the law of gravity, the power of grace lifts the believer high above every limitation by overriding the power of sin, flesh, and Satan. If you are intimidated at the prospect of resisting the outside forces, keep in mind the extent to which the Spirit of God is more powerful. As such, Paul directs believers to rely solely on the Spirit for daily living: "So I say, *walk by the Spirit*, and *you will not gratify* the desires of the flesh. For the flesh desires what is contrary to the Spirit, and the Spirit what is contrary to the flesh. They conflict with each other so that you are not to do whatever you want. But if you are led by the Spirit, you are *not under the law*" (Galatians 5:16–18).

The new life simply calls for the believer to *walk by the Spirit*, and in the process, the *desires of the flesh* will not have power over our lives. In other words, walking by the Spirit automatically overrides the forces that influence sinful actions. However, although this is good news for those who are trying with all their strength to avoid sin, we are called to a far greater way of life than merely avoiding sinful behaviors. The beauty of Christ living through us is that we have the opportunity to attract more people to Jesus. Therefore, walking by the Spirit not only keeps us from sinning but also produces spiritual fruit that reveals the light of God to the world. As Paul stated to the Ephesians, "For you were once darkness, but now *you are light* in the Lord. Live as children of light" (Ephesians 5:8–9).

If you are still hesitant to release your grip on rules-based living, keep in mind that if we are led by the Spirit, we are *not under the law.* Those who live under the law can operate based on only human strength. However, there is no need for external rules any longer because the believer is now influenced by the internal work of the Holy Spirit. Despite this spiritual truth, many people still fall into the trap of applying new rules to their lives that define the fruit of the Spirit. Many verses in the Bible describe the qualities of the Spirit, but we must not approach these verses as another list of rules or we will continue to operate based on human strength. It helps to remember that believers are not merely seeking assistance from the Spirit to reach a higher standard of excellence. Instead, we are completely enabled to rise above carnal living based on the overriding desires, motivations, and yearnings that come only from the Spirit.

The final piece of the puzzle is learning how to walk by the Spirit. This comes back to the important role our minds play in daily living. Our minds are the control center of our lives and ultimately dictate how we live. The thoughts we choose to entertain drive our feelings, attitudes, and actions. Therefore, as we develop a mind-set that focuses on the lust of the flesh, the lust of the eyes, and the pride of life, we will walk in the flesh. As we develop a mind-set that focuses on the things of the Spirit, we will walk by the Spirit. Paul addresses the importance of our thought life in his letter to the Romans: "Those who live according to the flesh have their *minds set* on what the flesh desires; but those who live in accordance with the Spirit have their *minds set* on what the Spirit desires. The *mind governed* by the flesh is death, but the *mind governed* by the Spirit is life and peace" (Romans 8:5–6).

We have every opportunity to focus on what makes us feel discouraged, hopeless, and tempted to sin. However, as we keep our eyes on Jesus, who is the living embodiment of the Word of God, we will walk by the Spirit. Jesus said, "The Spirit gives life; the flesh counts for nothing. The *words I have spoken* to you— they are full of the Spirit and life" (John 6:63).

If you are tired of living defeated, I encourage you to start renewing your mind to the finished work of Christ. Take the time to grasp how wide and long and high and deep God's love applies to your life. Read the Word of God and immerse your thoughts in sound teaching that is centered on the grace of God. You must come to the unshakable theological understanding that you are perfectly righteous at the core (new creation), fully accepted as a child of God (intimate relationship), and live in a perpetual state of forgiveness (total forgiveness). Renewing your mind to the incredible blessings of the new covenant and following the grace-based spiritual growth process will produce a resurgence of love, joy, and peace that you cannot manufacture on your own.

Chapter 10

BRAND STORY

The most powerful person in the world is the storyteller.
STEVE JOBS[18]

MARKETERS USE A STRATEGY called *brand story* to form a compelling narrative that brings together the elements of the brand into one cohesive story that resonates with an audience. Storytelling is one of the most powerful communication tools because it creates an experience that causes people to connect emotionally to the subject of the story. Therefore, a brand story is more than simply telling the chronological history of the brand. Instead, it uses the common elements of storytelling, such as characters, settings, plots, conflict, and resolution, to make the audience believe the brand can truly impact their lives. As the audience feels a strong connection with the main character of the story, a sense of trust with the storyteller is created.

In 2006, Blake Mycoskie, a young serial entrepreneur, was traveling through Argentina when he ran across a woman who was part of a nonprofit shoe drive. The woman explained to him the devastating impact that many children experienced who could not afford shoes. The children were exposed to various diseases and had trouble going to school and getting water from the local well. Blake visited some of the villages and learned more about the challenges the nonprofit had in securing enough donations. He was deeply moved by his experience and immediately went to work searching for a better solution.

In relatively short order, Blake came up with the idea to create a for-profit shoe business that could consistently generate and control inventory for the children. The concept was built on the promise to give away a pair of shoes for every pair of shoes that was sold. Blake worked with local designers to create a shoe style that was common in Argentina but also modified for the American market. He named the company TOMS Shoes, which has since donated over ninety-five million shoes to children in need and has grown to an approximate value of $625 million. It was the company's brand story that generated huge interest and gave consumers the feeling of doing good every time they purchased a pair of shoes.

Other companies use a collection of short stories to create one cohesive narrative about the brand. Imagine a father who is overwhelmed by the memory of his daughter growing up. It's hard for him to believe that she's old enough to drive. It seems like just yesterday he took the training wheels off her banana-seat bike. Now she will be driving on the roads without any parental supervision. The father knows that motor vehicle accidents are the number one killer of teens, so he purchased a new vehicle with the highest safety ratings. Isn't that what any good parent would do? As he watches his little girl drive away down the winding country road for the first time, one four-letter word appears on the television screen. Love.

You may have seen similar advertisements from Subaru over the years. In 2008, the company launched the Love campaign that has resulted in a series of short stories that often play on the heartstrings of parents. There's no need to mention features like all-wheel drive, leather seating, or automatic high beams with the Love campaign. Subaru is not selling a vehicle in their advertisements; they are selling the value of love. Their collection of short stories attracts people who are passionate about their families, the outdoors, and life in general. The company has since used the campaign to create one cohesive brand story.

When it comes to creating an effective brand story, the subject of love is the most powerful message because it has universal appeal. When the world put together the first live global television broadcast on June 25, 1967, the Beatles wrote and performed their classic hit song "All You Need Is Love" specifically for this occasion. What better message to convey to over four hundred million people in twenty-six countries who came together for the first time over the airwaves? With over 183 million album sales, the Beatles are the best-selling music artists of all time. However, despite the countless songs, movies, and books that convey the message of love, only one story keeps topping the charts every year—the story of God's love.

With over six billion copies printed since the year 1815, the Bible is hands down the best-selling book of all time. There is simply no other story that can rival the heartbreak, romance, and passion that is revealed in the brand story of the gospel. Contrary to popular opinion, the Bible is not an instruction manual for life. Instead, it represents a cohesive story that reveals God's love for humanity. The story begins with God creating humankind to form a love relationship that would last forever. Tragically, the people chose to reject God and go their own way, which resulted in the devastating consequences of eternal separation from their Creator. In response, God went to the most extreme lengths possible to reconcile humanity to Himself and save people from certain destruction. The brand story of the gospel can be summarized in one simple yet powerful statement: *God loves you.*

The narrative of the gospel is still being written today as more people respond to God's love. But some refuse to believe in what they cannot visibly see. It's important to understand that everyone experiences doubt, but it's how we respond to doubt that has lasting implications. Just three years prior to the crucifixion, the disciples left everything in their lives to follow Jesus. They grew in faith as they watched Him drive out demons, heal the sick, and raise people from the dead. It's safe to say that the disciples held to the common Jewish belief that the Messiah would be established as the next political ruler of Israel. However, God had different plans that rocked the disciples to their core and ultimately put them in a season of doubt, sorrow, and confusion. The last thing in the world the disciples expected to see was the public execution of their Messiah, who was supposed to reign as the new king of Israel.

There are times when our expectations are so crushed that we may even question the existence of God. You may have experienced a painful divorce, the loss of a child, or the terminal illness of a loved one. However, God will not allow us to wallow in doubt for the remainder of our lives. After Jesus rose from the dead, He made a series of private appearances to the disciples to give them unwavering confidence in His divinity. As news spread that Jesus was alive, you can imagine the exhilaration of His closest followers. However, one person, Thomas, simply refused to believe it was true. After hearing the good news from the other disciples, Thomas insisted that he needed to see Jesus in the flesh before he would believe. "*Unless I see* the nail marks in his hands and put my finger where the nails were, and put my hand into his side, *I will not believe*" (John 20:25).

Some people refuse to believe the brand story of the gospel based on the "I'll believe it when I see it" argument. However, God knows when our desire for the truth is genuine and when we are simply playing mental gymnastics. Every fair-minded person must follow the evidence and make an informed decision about Christ. In this case, one week after Thomas expressed his doubts, Christ appeared to him risen from the dead. Jesus said to Thomas, "Put your finger here; *see my hands*. Reach out your hand and put it into my side. Stop doubting and believe" (John 20:27). God is always gracious to renew our faith when we experience seasons of perplexity. However, we are reminded that more than enough evidence exists to believe that Jesus is God, even for those who haven't seen Him in the flesh. "Because you have seen me, you have believed; blessed are those *who have not seen* and yet have believed" (John 20:29).

Some will say that only uneducated people could believe they are loved by an invisible God. I agree that we should not base our lives on anything that does not stand against intellectual scrutiny. However, the brand story of the gospel is the only worldview that can adequately address every possible intellectual, experiential, and moral consideration. Therefore, people are not being honest when they create unrealistic demands, such as seeing God in the flesh before they believe because by rejecting Jesus, they are putting their faith in an alternative worldview that cannot survive the intellectual, experiential, and moral tests. In addition, we know that rejecting Christ cannot be the result of lack of evidence because, at the end of the day, if you want to know that God exists, Jesus promises to reveal Himself. "Ask and it will be given to you; seek and you will find; knock and the door will be opened to you" (Matthew 7:7).

I can tell you from personal experience that you don't need to see someone in the flesh to know his or her love is real. Although I have never seen my biological mother, I have full confidence that she loves me. My confidence is not based on wishful thinking, and I don't see the world through rose-colored glasses. On the contrary, I am certain that my biological mother loves me based on three pieces of undeniable evidence.

In what the social workers described as an unusual request during the adoption process, my mother left behind three personal items that were placed in a bank safe for me to receive once I became an adult. Each of the following three items worked in sequential order to give me confidence that my biological mother loves me despite never having seen her in the flesh: a *professional portrait*, an *oil painting*, and a *handwritten letter*.

The Professional Portrait

I first opened the professional portrait of my mother when I was twenty years old. Having never seen a blood relative before, I sat in silence for ten minutes just looking at the image. At first, I was struck by her beauty and the vibrancy in her eyes. Knowing the mental health challenges that were part of her life, perhaps I feared seeing a woman in distress, but the life in her eyes put my mind at ease. As I continued to study the photograph, my interest turned to the family resemblance. It may seem strange to those who have always known their biological relatives, but seeing my reflection in the image of my mother was a deeply impactful experience. I realized at that moment how the physical attributes we share with our relatives are a powerful reminder that we come from people who existed before us.

In the same way, as we study the world around us, we will see evidence that we ultimately come from a living Being who has existed in eternity past. We know from basic observation that life always comes from life. Plant life always comes from plant life. Animal life always comes from animal life. Human life always comes from human life. Since the evidence confirms that life never comes from nonlife, we must logically conclude that human life originated from a living Being. We may not have the ability to see the invisible God, but we can see our reflections in His eternal existence. The brand story of the gospel supports this evidence by tracing the origin of human life back to God. "Then the Lord God formed a man from the dust of the ground and *breathed into his nostrils the breath of life*, and the man became a living being" (Genesis 2:7).

Based on the evidence of human origin, the next logical observation is that human life must have intrinsic value. The value of humanity cannot come from the subjective opinions of other people when it has been ascribed based on the virtue of being created in the image of God. As a result, we have an objective basis to demand the proper treatment of every human life. However, if we say that God does not exist, we must also maintain that human value is based on the subjective opinions of other people. This creates a slippery moral slope that is often used to justify immoral behavior in the name of advancing an agenda. At the end of the day, whoever holds the most power in any given situation will often find a way to justify the mistreatment of other people, whether that applies to the rapist, abortionist, or communist dictator, or whether that applies to people who engage in less egregious activities, such as marginalizing a coworker to win the promotion.

We all have a deep sense of knowing that human life has intrinsic value because the evidence that God exists is built into our internal consciences. It's for this reason we hold the newborn baby with great care and help the elderly find comfort in their final years. When we see the grave mistreatment of suppressed people around the world, we experience moral outrage, knowing that they have intrinsic value. Although we can choose to ignore our consciences, we see the reflection of the invisible God in our internal compass that affirms the value of human life. The brand story of the gospel shows that humans have incalculable value based on the sacrifice God was willing to make to rescue humanity. "For God so loved the world that *he gave his one and only Son*, that whoever believes in him shall not perish but have eternal life" (John 3:16).

The evidence that humanity reflects the image of God also extends to our innate sense of purpose in life. The notion that God does not exist would mean that we are merely random collocations of atoms that came into existence by accident. If we believe the universe is accidental, which would also mean that our existence is accidental, then we must logically conclude that what we do with our lives has no ultimate meaning. Although we might have a strong feeling that our lives have purpose, such as raising a family or traveling the world, we must admit that we have constructed an illusion in our minds. However, once again, we have a deep sense of knowing that our lives do have meaning, which is more evidence that we were created for a purpose.

The brand story of the gospel affirms that our purpose is found in bringing glory to God. "I have *brought you glory* on earth by finishing the work you gave me to do" (John 17:4).

The Oil Painting

When I first opened the oil painting, I was struck by the primary colors and abstract style that was in common practice during the time I was born. The painting had the look of a sun rising halfway above a mountain range that extended horizontally across the canvas. The top part of the painting depicted the optimism of a bright and expansive morning sky. There was also an abstract feeling to several of the more subtle features in the painting, such as what looked like the morning fog that floated off the mountain and a red blotch that could have represented a rock wall. The overall impression of the painting seemed to express the hopeful beginning of a new day.

One night after the painting had been leaning against the wall for several months, I began to see the abstract elements from a completely different perspective. I realized the mountain range was a woman on her back and the sun rising was her pregnant womb. The mountains were built on a platform that was the bed. The morning fog cascading off the mountainside was the woman's hair. The red blotch was in the precise location of the human heart. The bottom of the mountain range even had the arch of a woman's back. Finally, of course, the sun immerging from the mountains represented the child being formed in the womb. I realized at that moment that my mother was expressing her love to me through the painting.

You don't have to search far to see the undeniable evidence that God has expressed His love to humanity through creation. We cannot mistake the order and beauty of the created world that has been designed specifically for our enjoyment. When it comes to the fundamental belief that God exists, the brand story of the gospel reveals that creation provides evidence that we come from a powerful, artistic, and benevolent Creator. "The heavens declare the glory of God; the skies proclaim the work of his hands. Day after day they pour forth speech; night after night they *reveal knowledge*" (Psalm 19:1–2).

King David's poetic language demonstrates that creation is God's way of speaking, or perhaps even shouting, that He exists. As thinking human beings, we are expected to follow the evidence that points to the divine Creator. We see the glory of God expressed in the oceans, mountains, and impressive display of wildlife. As we marvel at the strength of the lion, elegance of the giraffe, and humor of the walrus, we are showing appreciation for the artistry, power, and brilliance of the Creator.

None of the created world would have been possible without an intelligent mind. The intricacy that is required for human life to exist is far too complicated to have happened by chance. Consider for a moment the sophistication that goes into building a camera lens. The process requires the work of talented designers, engineers, and manufacturers. No thinking person would ever claim that camera lenses come into being by accident. As we travel from the camera lens to the human eye, we understand that the human eye is far more complex. Therefore, how can we say that the camera lens requires a designer while insisting the human eye does not? In the same way the oil painting reveals the artistic mind of my mother, creation provides more than enough evidence that an intelligent mind put the universe together.

The Handwritten Letter

I waited several days to open the handwritten letter from my mother. Although the first two items were important to get a general feeling about her, I knew the letter would provide the best insights into her thoughts. My mother started the letter with sincere regret that her life was too complicated to properly care for me. It was clear that she thought deeply about her decision to give me up for adoption and wanted to provide me with the best life possible. It was important for me to understand in her own words the reason she put me up for adoption. The letter also provided insights that had an enormous impact on my life many years later. I am grateful that she made the effort to express her thoughts to me in written form. I always knew that my mother existed, but it was the handwritten letter that offered the most clarity into her heart.

In the same way, anthropology shows that most people around the world believe in the existence of God. However, the belief that God exists does not answer the most important questions about life. What does God say about why we were created, how we are supposed to live, and what happens after we die? People throughout history have tried to answer these questions, but their efforts have resulted in numerous contradictory theories. The truth is that nobody can figure out what God is thinking unless He speaks to us directly. The apostle John reminds us that Jesus is the handwritten letter that reveals the specific thoughts of God: "The *Word became flesh* and made his dwelling among us. We have seen his glory, the glory of the one and only Son, who came from the Father, full of grace and truth" (John 1:14).

Jesus made the audacious claim not merely to speak the thoughts of God but that He was, in fact, God in human form. In other words, if we want to know exactly who God is and what God thinks, we must listen to Jesus. Considering the different world religions and opinions about God, how can we be certain that Jesus is the real deal? In short, we can discern that Jesus is the most credible option based on testimony from eyewitnesses who wrote down the events that transpired throughout His public ministry. Specifically, we will examine four attributes that elevate Jesus far above every other purveyor of God: the *teachings of Jesus*, the *lifestyle of Jesus*, the *way Jesus died*, and the *resurrection of Jesus* from the dead.

The Teachings of Jesus

Even the most hardened skeptics must concede that Jesus was a brilliant teacher. He was a master storyteller who made challenging concepts easy to understand. However, the power of His teachings extends well beyond just technique. Jesus introduced revolutionary concepts that are still being practiced today by people who don't even believe in Him, such as *turn the other cheek* and *treat others the way you want to be treated.* Unfortunately, there have been many people with delusions of deity over the centuries, but the teachings of Jesus don't sound like the words from a person who needed psychiatric help. On the contrary, when we study the words of Jesus, we find that He was nothing short of an ethical genius.

The people who saw and heard Jesus teach in the first century were amazed that He had so much wisdom without having received any formal training. People tend to place confidence in teachers based on their level of education. However, Jesus wanted the people to understand that His teachings had great insights because they came directly from God. He told the crowds, "My teaching is not my own. It comes from the one who sent me" (John 7:16). Also, the scribes always taught based on the authority of Scripture, but Jesus often appealed to Himself as the authority of His teachings. "You have heard that it was said, 'Eye for eye, and tooth for tooth.' *But I tell you*, do not resist an evil person. If anyone slaps you on the right cheek, turn to them the other cheek also" (Matthew 5:38–39).

Jesus knew the people were astonished by His teachings, so He presented them with a special challenge. Anybody who wanted to know if His teachings really came from God had one way to find out—try them on for size and watch what happens. He told the people, "Anyone who chooses to do the will of God will find out whether my teaching comes from God or whether I speak on my own" (John 7:17). First-century eyewitnesses had never seen or heard anybody teach with such insight, wisdom, and authority, and no teacher has come close ever since.

The Lifestyle of Jesus

Imagine during the next presidential campaign the two candidates square off during a nationally televised debate. After a series of policy discussions, the debate gets heated as the candidates question each other's moral character. How would the crowd respond if one of the candidates claimed to have lived a perfectly moral life? The audience would likely throw tomatoes at the candidate, who would probably lose the election in a landslide. We need to interview only a few people from the candidate's past to uncover many interesting moral failures.

However, I find it fascinating that no tomatoes were thrown at Jesus when He made the same claim. One day Jesus stood among a group of people, including some of His enemies, and asked the most astonishing question. "Can any of you prove me guilty of sin?" (John 8:46). Amazingly, nobody stepped forward to make an honest claim that Jesus had sinned. Instead, even His enemies in the crowd remained silent. The way Jesus lived should garner the admiration of every truth seeker. He did not allow the cultural customs and prejudices to deter Him from loving people, associate with Samaritans, and respect the dignity of women. Jesus lived a perfectly moral life.

The Way Jesus Died

What a person truly values will come to the surface during their final moments before dying. Jesus did not have a peaceful experience with family and friends in a comfortable environment before taking His last breath. He was gruesomely beaten and abused, both physically and psychologically, for several hours before being slammed against a wooden cross. The Roman soldiers stood around and mocked Jesus as He hung naked and unrecognizable. I don't know about you, but if something like that even came close to happening to me, I would probably curse my enemies.

However, words can't describe the moral capacity to love that Jesus showed on the cross. When everything was on the line and Jesus experienced His moment of crisis, He practiced what He preached by extending the most profound gesture of love the world has ever seen. "Father, forgive them, for they do not know what they are doing" (Luke 23:34). When people understand the magnitude of Christ's love He demonstrated toward His enemies while dying on the cross, those who really want to know God must respond as the centurion officer who witnessed these events unfold: "Surely He was the Son of God!" (Matthew 27:54).

The Resurrecting of Jesus

Jesus had many impressive qualities, but nothing was more significant than His bodily resurrection from the dead. The resurrection of Christ stands alone as the most powerful and conclusive piece of evidence that affirms the credibility of Jesus. He promised eternal life to anyone who believes in Him and backed it up with an historical resurrection from the dead. Paul was so confident in the veracity of the resurrection that he hinged the entire Christian faith on that one singular event. "And if Christ has not been raised, your faith is futile; you are still in your sins" (1 Corinthians 15:17). In short, the historical resurrection of Christ from the dead served to vindicate His claims that He is the way, the truth, and the life.

To underscore the truthfulness of this historical event, consider what happened after the disciples saw Jesus risen from the dead. James, the younger brother of Jesus, did not believe his brother was the Messiah until after he saw the risen Christ. Thomas was not willing to believe anymore until after he saw Jesus risen. Peter, who just days earlier had denied knowing Jesus because he was terrified at the prospect of being persecuted, transformed into a bold preacher of the gospel. In fact, all of the disciples became faithful missionaries for the remainder of their lives after seeing Christ risen from the dead. The disciples did not die martyrs' deaths based on what they believed. Instead, they were willing to die based on what they claimed to have seen—the dead Christ risen!

The brand story of the gospel is the only worldview that stands against every intellectual, experiential, and moral consideration. Although we tend to overcomplicate its simple message, the Bible is our heavenly Father's handwritten love letter that is calling us home.

Come Home

My mother included one unexpected notation in her handwritten letter to me. She requested that I find my three biological siblings and provided their names and birth dates. However, her request went against my desires at the time because I was loyal to the family that had adopted me. I tried to run away from her request and suffered through many deep-rooted wounds for the next fifteen years that could have been resolved much sooner. In the same way, many people have read the handwritten letter from heaven but still refuse to come home. In the process, their attempts to mask their cosmic sense of isolation and search for true love has come up empty. If you are willing to open your heart to God, your search for love will be fulfilled.

Jesus is calling you home. He is the lover of your soul, the place you belong, and the purpose for your life. If you have not accepted Jesus as your personal Savior, please consider putting your trust in Him today. He is calling you home right now and is waiting to receive you into His arms. If you have accepted Jesus as your personal Savior, may you set your light on the lampstand of true spiritual freedom so that more people may know Him.

Notes

1. Anastasiya Golovatenko, "Six Myths About PR For Your Business," *Entrepreneur*, January 5, 2017, https://www.entrepreneur.com/article/287313.

2. Nicholas Confessore and Karen Yourish, "$2 Billion Worth of Free Media for Donald Trump," *The New York Times*, March 15, 2016, https://www.nytimes.com/2016/03/16/upshot/measuring-donald-trumps-mammoth-advantage-in-free-media.html.

3. "Apple Reinvents the Phone with iPhone," Apple, January 9, 2007, https://www.apple.com/newsroom/2007/01/09Apple-Reinvents-the-Phone-with-iPhone/.

4. Kedran Whitten, "How to Adjust Your Marketing Budget During a Pandemic," *Nashville Business Journal*, September 29, 2020, https://www.bizjournals.com/nashville/news/2020/09/29/how-to-adjust-your-marketing-budget-during-a-pandemic.html.

5. William Arruda, "The Most Damaging Myth About Branding," *Forbes*, September 6, 2016, https://www.forbes.com/sites/williamarruda/2016/09/06/the-most-damaging-myth-about-branding/?sh=119d98765c4f.

6. "Old Spice: Smell Like A Man, Man," Widen+Kenney, February 2020, https://www.wk.com/work/old-spice-smell-like-a-man-man/.

7. Robin Grant, "Widen+Kennedy's Old Spice Case Study," We Are Social, August 10, 2010, https://wearesocial.com/uk/blog/2010/08/wieden-kennedys-spice-case-study.

8. "Christians: More Like Jesus or Pharisees?" Barna, June 3, 2013, https://www.barna.com/research/christians-more-like-jesus-or-pharisees/.

9. Asad Meah, "35 Inspirational Howards Schultz Quotes On Success," Awaken The Greatness Within, March 7, 2020, https://www.awakenthegreatnesswithin.com/35-inspirational-howard-schultz-quotes-on-success/.

10. "Our Culture: Move Fast. Be Bold. Be Yourself.," Facebook Careers, https://www.facebook.com/careers/facebook-life/.

11. Ross Kimbarovsky, "Marketing Is About Values," Crowdspring, August 31, 2010, https://www.crowdspring.com/blog/marketing-values/.

12. Jim Edwards, "Dominos Admits Pizza Was 'the Worst'; Bets the Company on Ads Vowing Change," *CBS News*, January 14, 2010, https://www.cbsnews.com/news/dominos-admits-pizza-was-the-worst-bets-the-company-on-ads-vowing-change/.

13. "Domino's Vision, Mission and Values," Domino's Pizza, https://www.dominos.co.nz/inside-dominos/corporate/vision-and-mission.

14. Richard Voreis, "Quotes for Business Success from Famous People: Warren Buffett and Branding," Dollars & Sense, July 15, 2020, https://dollarsandsense.usglassmag.com/quotes-for-business-success-from-famous-people-warren-buffett-and-branding/.

15. flipbeanso2, "Steve Jobs' reaction to this insult shows why he was such a great CEO," DailyMotion, 2016, https://www.dailymotion.com/video/x3as250.

16. Ananya Bhattacharya, "5 Great Elon Musk Quotes on Innovation," Inc., March 20, 2015, https://www.inc.com/ananya-bhattacharya/5-elon-musk-quotes-about-innovation.html.

17. "About Us," Nestle, https://www.nestle.com/aboutus.

18. Jay Yarow, "Here's An Awesome Story About Steve Jobs Telling An Employee He's Going To Become The World's Best Story Teller In 1994," *Business Insider*, July 3, 2013, https://www.businessinsider.com/steve-jobs-story-teller-2013-7.

About the Author

Robert Wachter is a speaker, faith-based coach, and founder and lead pastor for Imagine Church, Washington State. As the former chief marketing officer for a real estate company that saw six billion dollars in annual sales during his tenure, Robert uses his experience across several dimensions to help others reach their full potential and make Jesus irresistible to people everywhere. Robert has been featured by radio and news outlets regarding his evangelistic approach to ministry.

Connect with Robert on Facebook, Instagram (@RobJWachter), and RobertWachter.com.

CPSIA information can be obtained
at www.ICGtesting.com
Printed in the USA
FSHW021619250821
83976FS